After reading *Faith Undaunted*, I can't help thinking of the elderly lady's reaction when she heard J. C. Ryle preach: 'He's no Bishop. I could understand every word!' And so ... Donald Macleod blesses us with his vintage clarity in this stirring, searching, sustaining apology for 'Apostles' Creed' faith.

Dale Ralph Davis
Respected Author and Old Testament Scholar

From time to time, books are written that manage to combine brevity with beauty, and clarity with comprehensiveness as they account for the great themes of the Christian gospel (C. S. Lewis' *Mere Christianity*, or Timothy Keller's *The Reason for God*, come to mind). Among them, Donald MacLeod's *Faith Undaunted* must now take its place. It surveys the major contours of basic Christian conviction, with simplicity and sympathy. It addresses the nature of faith; its reasons, and its grounds. It outlines the central tenets of Apostolic Christianity, and focusses with special lucidity on the person and work of Christ. It deals kindly yet firmly with common missteps and confusions about the nature of the Christian life, the character and claims of truth, and the place of reason, faith, and experience. It does not discount the church, but celebrates and commends her to every believer in Jesus. And it calls us all to take up our cross and to follow the lead of the Good Shepherd Himself on the path of discipleship, even though it will requires us all to walk some day through 'death's dark vale'. Every Christian will benefit from this delightful book. But as a guide to the basics of the faith for new disciples it should prove invaluable.

David Strain
Senior Minister of First Presbyterian Church, Jackson, Mississippi
Author of *Ruth & Esther: There is a Redeemer and Sudden Reversals*

FAITH
Undaunted

Embracing Faith and Knowledge
in a Post-Truth Era

DONALD MACLEOD

CHRISTIAN
FOCUS

Copyright © Donald Macleod 2022

Hardback ISBN 978-1-5271-0901-8
Ebook ISBN 978-1-5271-0949-0

10 9 8 7 6 5 4 3 2 1

Published in 2022
by
Christian Focus Publications Ltd,
Geanies House, Fearn, Ross-shire,
IV20 1TW, Great Britain.

www.christianfocus.com

Cover design by
Pete Barnsley

Printed and bound by
Bell & Bain, Glasgow

Contents

✟ FOREWORD ✟

Here is a book that deserves a wide readership and careful attention in a day when it has become commonplace to assume that faith has been seriously dented and almost demolished by the modern 'scientific' view of the world.

So it is assumed. But far from being demolished, having 'faith' is apparently alive and well. On a daily basis people who demean a theistic and Christian worldview confidently formulate their own creeds: 'I believe in Evolution as the Creator of all things', or 'My faith is shaped by Science as the final explanation', or even the remarkable conviction about the origin of the cosmos, 'I believe in Gravity'. The problem of course is that none of these objects of faith has creative power to bring something out of nothing. And it remains as true today as it was in the days of the Greek thinker Parmenides that 'from nothing comes nothing'.

Yet the frequent and often unreflective use of the words 'I believe in ...' simply underlines that faith, whatever its object, is basic to our lives. Believing certain things to be true, trusting certain truth claims, or certain people, and acting on the basis of that 'faith' is part and parcel of what it means to be human. There is no escape from having a basic creed with basic presuppositions and confessing it in the way we live, whether we do it deliberately and consciously or otherwise. The idea that there are 'people of faith' who constitute a subset of the human race is a fallacy. We are all 'people of faith'. The real issue is the content and nature of that faith.

That is why Donald Macleod's book *Faith Undaunted* is as welcome as it is important. It is *important* because the issue of what we believe is fundamental to life, profoundly influences our character, and shapes the way we live. It is *welcome* because its author belongs to that special class of writers who have been gifted with both exceptional intellectual ability and a writing style that throbs with both energy and clarity. In these pages he invites us to sit down with him, as it were, as he explains how he himself completes the sentence beginning 'I believe ...'.

Gifted intellectuals who make a Christian profession can be found in all the disciplines – in the sciences, literature, medicine, law, high culture, and not least, but in some ways most intriguingly, in philosophy. But perhaps in the interests of full disclosure it should be said at the outset (for any reader who may not already know), Professor Macleod is a Christian theologian. But if you draw premature conclusions from this fact, you will soon discover that he will not only disarm you but also intrigue you in a way that will compel you to read on. You will then be invited to think patiently and clearly with him about what has often been regarded as the greatest and most fundamental question of all: Why is there something and not nothing?

That question continues to haunt thinking people because so many of the oft-repeated answers given to it are intellectually facile. For people who deny the existence of a personal God who is the loving Creative Genius do not seem to be able to avoid replacing him with a false and impersonal deity bearing sophisticated title yet still incapable of bringing something out of nothing.

It may be that as you follow the argument of these pages, you will encounter a few unfamiliar names from the past. There is no need to fear, however. For Professor Macleod not only identifies these individuals were but also explains the nature of their influence on the times in which we live. *Faith Undaunted* is thus educational at more than one level. And if at any point it stretches readers they will soon feel the benefit of the exercise.

Donald Macleod's contention that the ancient Christian confession 'I believe in God ...' cannot be easily dismissed is surely right, as was unintentionally illustrated by an event reported some years ago in *The Telegraph*. Its report of the memorial service for the English novelist Sir Kingsley Amis recorded that his son Martin prompted much merriment when he recounted a conversation between his father and the Russian playwright and poet Yevgeni Yevtushenko. Perhaps assuming all Englishmen regarded themselves by definition as 'Christians', Yevtushenko asked Amis if it was true that he was in fact *an atheist*. Kingsley Amis's response was revealing: 'I'm an atheist, yes. But it's more that: *I hate him*.'

Perhaps the amused congregation did not reflect long enough to recognise that the apparent contradiction was in fact a profound self-revelation. The self-identifying atheist had no way of escape from 'I believe ...'. Perhaps too the laughter of some of England's elites was hollow, caused by an unnerving echo of Amis's words sounding in their own hearts. In any event his unguarded confession of hatred underlines the inescapable significance of the theme of these pages.

So, if you are already a 'believer' you will find here much here to stimulate and help. And if you are not, I hope you will have the needed intellectual integrity and moral courage to read on. In either case you will see why the subject of this little book is important and why its publication is so welcome.

Sinclair B. Ferguson

✛ INTRODUCTION ✛

As a young Christian, I heard a great deal about the dangers of 'head knowledge' and, linked to this, the idea that the greatest danger facing Christianity was 'learning' and the scholars who practised and purveyed it. Intellect was dangerous; faith was a matter of the heart, not of the mind, and the heart could get along perfectly well without the dogmas.

Such sentiments were then widespread throughout Evangelicalism, and, in their own way, they were a comfort. Faith could dispense with intellectual justification. But then, when I discovered such works as J. G. Machen's *Christianity and Liberalism* (1923), the companion volume, *What Is Faith?*, and the massively erudite writings of B. B. Warfield, I had my eureka moment: suspicion of intellect, and impatience with doctrines, was the hallmark, not of Evangelicalism, but of the very Liberalism that Christian orthodoxy deplored. Modernism had many varieties, but common to all of them was the belief that piety was first and foremost a matter of experience and feeling; that Christianity was not primarily a belief system but a collection of 'values;' that it was the 'life' that mattered, and that the life could be lived regardless of what people believed.

Paradoxically, scholarship, as represented by 'the makers of modern theology,' had been used to drive a wedge between Christian discipleship and the long and distinguished tradition of Christian learning.

Then, as the century moved on, another paradigm took hold of the public mind: relativism. In its most radical form, it meant that there was no such thing as truth; more modestly, it meant that we couldn't be sure of anything. Certainty was arrogance, especially on such matters as the details of Jesus' life and the core principles of Christian ethics. Truth might be truth for me; it was not truth for anyone else, and this attitude soon began to make its presence felt even in Evangelical circles, particularly among students and the growing number of Evangelical academics. As G. K. Chesterton put it, 'What we suffer from today is humility in the wrong place. Modesty has settled on the organ of conviction, where it was never meant to be. A man was meant to be doubtful about himself, but undoubting about the truth; this has been exactly reversed.'[1]

This little book is not the story of a journey. It is a statement of where I've arrived, and why; and, while painfully conscious that I know only in part (1 Cor. 13:12), yet I can joyfully make my own the words of Hebrews 11:1: 'Faith is the assurance of things hoped for, the conviction of things unseen' (ESV). I am sure of the Invisible, sure of what He has done, and sure that what He has promised will one day be done.

---

1.   G. K. Chesterton, *Orthodoxy: A personal philosophy* (1908. Reprinted Fontana Books, 1961), p. 31.

1

✟ THE 'SENSE' OF DEITY ✟

All my life I've believed in God. That may sound like a dangerous admission. Does it not immediately confirm the suspicion that religious belief is a matter of historical accident: of early upbringing, perhaps, or even, at its crudest, a desire to please your parents? That argument cuts both ways, of course. Atheism, too, can be learned at your mother's knee. But even so, my admission suggests that I did not come to faith in God by way of rational argument and careful examination of the evidence.

To that charge, I must immediately plead guilty. I believed in God long before I ever heard of the so-called theistic proofs which, from the days of Thomas Aquinas (1225–1274) have been wheeled out to prove that there is 'a god'. But in this I am not alone. Few people, if any, have come to faith in God as the result of a long and rigorous process of philosophical reasoning, and the Bible itself never sets out to prove that God exists. Instead, it takes Him for granted, simply announcing, 'In the beginning, God ...' and then going on to account for what it sees as the real mystery: not the existence of God, but the existence of the universe. According to the psalmist, the heavens declare the glory of God (Ps. 19:1), but that doesn't mean that they are the proof that He exists, far less that they are the proof that He 'probably' exists. The psalmist assumes that God exists, and what the heavens declare, in their ever-expanding complexity and beauty, is not that He exists, but that He is glorious.

The New Testament adopts the same starting point. The Apostle John begins his gospel with words which echo the opening words of Genesis, 'In the beginning was the Word'; and St Paul begins his exposition of the gospel in the *Epistle to the Romans*, not by trying to prove that God exists, but by declaring that He has revealed Himself within every human being (Rom. 1:19). God gives Himself visibility through the things that He has made, and thus causes His eternal power and God-ness to be clearly seen.

At the same time, Paul is fully aware that this revelation by itself never leads to true piety. Instead, human beings invariably suppress and pervert it. In the case of the vast majority, this means that they descend into idolatry and false religions, but in the case of a minority, it means denying that there is any deity at all. Either way, says the apostle, we are without excuse. We have all received revelation, we have all understood it, and when, at the Judgment, God challenges us as to what we did with it, He will be perfectly within His rights.

John Calvin built on the foundation laid by St Paul when he declared that a 'sense of deity' was engraved on every heart and the 'seed of religion' sown in every soul; and it is this universal sense of deity that explains the worldwide incidence of religion. 'There is no nation so barbarous, no people so savage,' writes Calvin (quoting Cicero), 'that they have not a deep-seated conviction that there is a God. And they who in other aspects of life seem least to differ from brutes still continue to retain some seed of religion.'[1] This is why every

---

1. John Calvin, *Institutes of the Christian Religion*, ed. John T. McNeill, tr. Ford Lewis Battles (Philadelphia: Westminster Press, 1960), I:III, 1.

society has its priests, its altars and its temples. These religions have almost invariably been great evils, but, even as such, they bear witness to mankind's universal awareness of God, and our need to deflect His displeasure by one means or another.

In the circumstances, then, the fact that from my earliest childhood I was surrounded by people who believed in God was not in the least unusual. Had I been brought up in India, Vietnam or Saudi Arabia the situation would have been the same. Nor was it even slightly unusual that, by the time I was a teenager, I took it for granted that I lived in a world that owed its existence to God.

Questioning our faith

But then neither is it unusual that at some point we begin to question this belief and start asking ourselves, 'Why do I believe? And can this faith be justified?' Nor is it unusual that such questionings can sometimes amount to an acute personal crisis in which all that we believe is cast into doubt; and perhaps the more assured our faith once was, the greater the crisis. It is not only a theory we have lost. We find ourselves being sucked into a world without light, meaning or hope: a world in which there is nothing to cling to, and nothing assured, and where, if we are logical, there is no reason to live by the Ten Commandments or the Golden Rule: a world where the best we could hope for would be to end up as fossils.

It's never very clear what causes such doubts. Humanists would like to argue that it is sudden exposure to modern science or philosophy or psychology or biblical criticism, or, perhaps, a dose of realism, as we suddenly realise how much evil there is in the world and ask, How could God (if there is a god) allow so much cruelty and mayhem?

It's probably true that such arguments can stir up serious challenges to faith, especially when they're deployed by charismatic figures who make it their mission in life to rescue young people from what they see as the baneful influence of religion. But the idea that doubt is always the product of rational argument, or of the rise of modern science, is a delusion. Many Christians fought personal battles with atheism long before Darwin, Freud or Strauss were ever heard of; and among these were some of the greatest figures in our Scottish theology, such as James Fraser of Brea, Thomas Halyburton and 'Rabbi' Duncan.

The Devil, of course, is no atheist, but he doesn't need science, psychology or social pressure to sow the seed of doubt. He can do it directly, and all by himself. All it takes is a thought out of the blue: an 'If'; or an 'Are you sure?'; or what looks like a word of wise counsel, such as, 'You really need to be sure about this.' Besides, he is adept at attaching our doubts to our personal neuroses. The more inclined we are to anxiety, the higher the level of certainty we need; and the more depressed we become over the theological bereavement we have suffered, the harder it is to comfort us.

Justifying our faith to ourselves

How then, once we're sucked into the vortex, can we ever justify our faith to ourselves?

But doesn't this very question immediately pose a difficulty? Should we not have found the reasons *before* we came to faith, not afterwards; otherwise, the arguments amount to no more than wishful thinking? We want God to exist, and then go looking for arguments to prove it.

The obvious reply to this is that it is no different from what happens in science, where the hypotheses (often the product of intuition) usually come before the proof,[2] and where the ensuing experiments are set up in the hope of finding it. A scientist may be convinced that his theory is true before he is able to provide any experimental verification, and even before he can work out what sort

---

2.   Cf. Einstein's comment, 'A new idea comes suddenly and in a rather intuitive way' (Walter Isaacson, *Einstein: His Life and Universe*; London: Simon and Schuster, 2007, p. 113).

of experiment it would take. This leaves him in the same position as the theologian who, starting with faith, looks for reasons. All ground-breaking theories began as unproven hypotheses.

For example, as early as 1915, Einstein's mathematics led him to formulate the Theory of General Relativity, but it was verified only four years later when photographs taken during a solar eclipse confirmed the existence of deflected starlight around the sun's mass. Of course, the evidence needed to prove a hypothesis in physics is quite different from the sort of evidence necessary to prove one in the field of religion (a fact too often forgotten), but there is, nonetheless, a fundamental similarity between the approach of the scientist and the approach of the theologian.

The theologian's approach was defined by Anselm when, away back in the eleventh century, he defined his life's work as 'faith seeking understanding' (*fides quaerens intellectum*). Theology was not an afterthought designed to persuade himself and others to believe. It was an attempt to give reasons for the faith he already had: in Anselm's case, a full-blown Christian faith.

How can we account for the faith we've had since childhood?

Having been once rattled, then, how can I account for the faith I have held since childhood?

First of all, by acknowledging that the account St Paul gives of our human awareness of God corresponds exactly to my own experience. The idea of God was always in my mind, and it was there, says the Apostle, because God had planted it there; and the very idolatries characteristic of the world's religions showed that this awareness was universal. Idolatry was not atheism, but the perversion of a deeply engrained theism. Every human, simply as such, is aware of the eternal power and God-ness (Rom. 1:20) of one on whom they are utterly dependent and to whom they will one day give account. This is why the whole world has built temples, prayed, and offered sacrifices. Conscience has made even the most decadent tremble; football's superstars cross themselves as they run out on to the pitch and gaze adoringly heavenward when they score a goal; in the moment of bereavement, even the most flippant of modern human beings seem convinced that their departed loved ones are looking down on them from heaven.

All of this accords with what we might expect in the light of Romans 1; when, years later, I came across John Calvin's exposition of St Paul, I recognised myself immediately in the person the Apostle and the Reformer were describing. The sense of deity had indeed been ascribed on my heart; God had planted the knowledge of Himself in the depths of my being; the Almighty had sown the seed of religion in my soul; and a voice within said, Bow down and worship.

This doesn't mean that as an infant of days I 'knew' any of this, any more than I knew that the sun rose and set, or that it was now two hours since my last meal or that it was wrong to demand that my mother instantly stop whatever she was doing and come and feed me. What it does mean is that, assuming I developed normally, I would come to know all such things. I would develop a sense of time and space, and long before I knew the word 'cause', I learned that every time I banged the table with my spoon, it would be followed by a noise. As I observed the world around and interacted with it, the seed of religion would grow in my heart. I would learn that land, sea and sky were very big, and that I was very small, and often helpless; when in trouble, I would cry to God like the mariners in Psalm 107 (Calvin thought they were pagans, but they still prayed) or the crew of the boat in which Jonah found a berth when he tried to run away from God. They were definitely pagans, and decent ones, but they knew that their only hope was to call on the God whose tempest had placed them in peril of their lives.

But I also learned that I had to behave in a certain way. Some things were right and some things were wrong, not only for me, but for everybody. I also knew that I would have to answer for what I did, not only to my parents, but to the one above them. I can't say I was ever scared of Him, or terrified that, if I did something bad, He would hit me. But it was important to please Him.

It is this implanted sense of deity that the Bible addresses. It assumes that we have such an awareness and that, even before we begin to read it, the seed of religion is already in our hearts in the shape of the instinct to revere and to pray. The Bible never contradicts the knowledge of Himself that God has already planted in our hearts. It builds on it, and, as I grew in knowledge of the Scriptures, I came to acquiesce wholeheartedly in the criterion of God-ness laid down by Anselm: 'God is that than whom a greater cannot be conceived.'[3]

---

3. Anselm, *Proslogion*, 2 (Anselm of Canterbury: *The Major Works*, ed. Brian Davies and G. R. Evans; New York: Oxford University Press, 1998), p. 87.

2

✦ THE BANKRUPTCY OF ✦ THE ALTERNATIVES

I happily admit, then, that St Paul's statement that every human being is by nature aware of God is an entirely apt description of my own experience. Many others, however, will emphatically deny that it is an apt description of theirs. There is no seed of religion, they say, in their hearts, or any sense of accountability to a deity; and in any case, 'We don't need Him: the idea of a creator is superfluous. There are perfectly valid alternatives.'

But when I began to reflect on these alternatives, they seemed to me utterly bankrupt.

One very basic definition of God is that He, or it, is whoever, or whatever, accounts for the existence of the universe, and on this, the Christian faith is clear. The universe was created by God, the Almighty Maker of Heaven and Earth. This, too, I have believed since childhood; and not only that He made it, but He had filled it with millions of life-forms. Later on, inevitably, I encountered alternative explanations for the existence of the world, and for a while they shook me. But what struck me was, firstly, how limited the alternatives were; and, secondly, how unconvincing. They are represented by many *-isms*, but in the last analysis there is only one basic question: What was there before there was a world? And to that question there are only three possible answers.

First, before there was a world there was Nothing. Before there was Anything, there was Nothing. The nothing-ness of this Nothing must be taken with absolute seriousness. There was no matter, no mass, no energy, no light, no gravity, no electro-magnetic field, no protein, no amino acid: nothing but nothing, and surely the ancients spoke truth when they said, 'Out of nothing, nothing comes' (*Ex nihilo nihil fit*). There was no one to make anything, and nothing to make it with: nothing, in terms of the Big Bang Theory, to bang; and no one to press the button. A mind seeking understanding cannot rest here.

The second possibility is that before there was a universe, and even before there was light, there was some form of self-existent matter, untouched and un-programmed by mind, and yet somehow containing in itself everything that was needed to produce the world as we know it today, although only after a bewildering series of accidents and countless billions of years. On the most plausible form of this theory, this mass exploded, and the rest is, quite literally, history: the fallout from the mindless explosion of inanimate matter, dispersing its rubbish ever further away from its point of origin. Every physical object in the universe, no matter how complex or how beautiful, is a by-product of this accident; so, too, is every life-form; and so, too, is the human species. Our brains are no more than part of the debris: our imaginations, our consciences, our sense of beauty, our outburst of moral outrage, are only biochemical precipitates. And our flights of intellect fare no better. The theories of Darwin and Einstein, the PhD of Richard Dawkins, the dramas of Shakespeare, the art of Da Vinci, the symphonies of Mozart, the poetry of Sorley MacLean, the lyrics of Bob Dylan, are all part of the debris, as is the fact that we enjoy them and the fact that we know that we enjoy them and the fact that we are aware of ourselves enjoying them. We, with all our hopes and fears, our loves and hates, our guilt and our grievings, and our occasional moments of genius, are no more than episodes in the history of star-dust.

The mind that seeks to understand can find no rest here. It would be the end of our law courts, our academies, our art galleries and even of our demos.

In the Beginning, God

But there remains a third possibility: 'In the Beginning, God' (Gen. 1:1). These are, surely, the greatest opening words in human literature. But what do they mean?

First, that in the Beginning, before ever there was a world, there was Life. Life itself never had a beginning. It was there from all eternity in the person of the Living God, and this is why we live in a world which not only teems with material objects, such as the stars, but which also teems with myriad forms of life, ranging from the cactus to the rose, and from the mollusc to man. Life gave life, and this same Life is also the source of all the energy systems with which the world is blessed. Gravity, solar energy, nuclear power, electro-magnetism, all derive their energy from the eternal power of the Living God.

Secondly, in the Beginning there was Love; and, like Life, this Love never had a beginning. It is, says the Apostle John, what God is (I John 4:8), and since *He* never had a beginning, Love never had a beginning.

But how, we may ask, could this be, before there was a universe to love? Was God not then a great eternal, self-contained Solitary, better described in such abstract terms as 'the Ground of Being', 'the Transcendent', than as a Heavenly Father? But this is to ignore the Christian doctrine of the Trinity. The Father was never without the Son and the Holy Spirit, and that relationship was, from eternity, one of love, sharing and mutual pleasure. They spoke, they cooperated, and each rejoiced in the other, recognising that none was greater and none was lesser, but that each shared in all the fulness of God.

In this Love, God was happy, and, precisely because He was Love, He wished to communicate Life to other forms of existence; and not only so, but to create other intelligent beings, made in His own image, with whom He could share His own eternal life, and who might share in the happiness of the Father, the Son and the Holy Spirit. This was why, in one of the boldest moves in the history of Christian theology, Jonathan Edwards repeatedly argued that happiness was the chief end of creation.[1] It was in sharing His happiness with His creatures that God would find ultimate satisfaction. From this point of view, we would be fully warranted in arguing that, in the Beginning, there was Happiness, and that His concern to widen its circle was the great motive behind God's work of creation (and also, of course, His work of redemption).

Thirdly, in the Beginning, there was Word (*Logos*). This is why, in the very first chapter of Genesis, we repeatedly read that 'God said'. But this was not the beginning of divine speech. God and His Son were communicating with each other from all eternity. Indeed, His Son was such a perfect self-expression of the Father that the Son Himself can be called God's 'Word' (John 1:1, 14). Such language all too quickly leads us to the limits of our understanding, partly because it combines the abstract notion of 'word' with the warm notion of 'son'; and partly because it portrays the Logos not only as both the speaker and the word spoken, but because it also portrays Him as the one spoken about.

What we can grasp, however, is that, before ever there was a world, there was Reason and Intelligence, not as abstractions, but

---

1. See, for example, his *Dissertation on the End for which God created the World* (*The Works of Jonathan Edwards*, 2 vols., 1834. Reprinted Edinburgh: Banner of Truth Trust, 1974, Vol. 1), pp. 94-121.

as qualities of the living and loving eternal Creator. Not only was there life, then, but it was intelligent life: life linked to the most sublime logic and to the most brilliant powers of imagination. This eternal living and loving Intelligence explains why we and the world are here: 'In wisdom hast thou made them all,' cries the psalmist (Ps. 104:24 KJV). Here, in this living and loving eternal Intelligence, are the conceptual powers and the strategic foresight to deliver what Matter by itself could never deliver; and to impose on Matter whatever form God chose.

He speaks, and it is done

But beside this lies another wonder: this living and loving Intelligence did not need another agency or instrument to give effect to its will. This Wisdom speaks, and when He speaks, His speech has the power of omnipotence. When He speaks, it is done. This is the invisible reality behind the great astrophysical, geophysical and biophysical processes which gave our world its current form and filled it with life. Sun, moon and stars; the great oceans and the towering mountain ranges; the bee and the buffalo: all were conceived in the divine mind and brought into being by His mere word.

At first sight, it seems odd that a word should have such power. How can one speak something into being? At the most mundane level, however, there is an analogy here with the power of human oratory: a power which, throughout history, has both raised up and pulled down the world's mightiest empires. But the greatest demonstration of the power of word appeared in the life and ministry of Jesus Christ, God's incarnate Son. He spoke, and the wind and the sea obeyed Him (Mark 4:35-41). He spoke, and the dead rose (John 11:43). He spoke, and the lame walked (John 5:8). Sometimes, the very thought, unspoken, was enough, as when He turned water into wine (John 2:6-10), fed five thousand people on five loaves and two fish (John 6:5-14), or healed a centurion's servant without even seeing the man or asking his name (Matt. 8:5-13).

We live in a world where things make sense

From Genesis to Revelation, then, God gives effect to His will by speaking His mind; and, precisely because the universe was made by the divine Word, it bears witness everywhere to the fact that it is the product of a living Intelligence. This, and this alone, can explain why we find ourselves living in a world that is cognitively friendly: a world where things make sense, and which reveals its secrets to the enquiring human mind. Wherever we look, we find laws and we find order and we find mathematical precision and we find the most remarkable balance of forces; when we can't find it, we're perplexed, and go looking for it; and when we do find it, we turn it to our technical advantage.

Then, at the other end of the scale, we learn that the air we breathe, the water we drink and the chairs we sit on are made up of trillions of tiny atoms attracting and repelling each other with bewildering complexity, but with a no less bewildering precision; and then the researchers tell us that, even within the atom, the force of gravity operates, and every atom is in effect a whole system within a system. Minuscule though it is, every particle not only contains its own secrets, but is willing to reveal them to us if we are prepared to look and listen. And when we turn our eyes to the biosphere, to the flora and fauna all around us, we find that, despite the vast variety of life-forms, they all have one thing in common: DNA, which both provides the building-blocks of life and distinguishes life from life. Here again, we find both order and complexity, and variety without randomness; here again, we find the same willingness to yield up secrets.

It is far beyond me to give any account of the wonders of astrophysics, nuclear physics or microbiology; and, sadly, those who *are* able to describe them too often attribute them to Nothing or to Blind Chance or to Pure Accident or, in the interests of persuasive rhetoric, to Nature. But it is hard to see how Nature can account for itself. Ever since Charles Darwin began to use the term beguilingly,

Mother Nature and Dame Nature have taken the place of the Baals and Asherahs of the ancient fertility cults. To the modern western mind, mountains and rhinos are far more interesting than their Creator, yet, however maternal and sagacious we make Nature out to be, 'She' has no agency. After all, as John C. Lennox points out, 'Nature' is no more than a name for 'every physical thing there is';[2] and it is hard to accept the hypothesis that 'every physical thing there is' owes its existence to 'every physical thing there is.' How did everything know where everything else should go?

A genome of extraordinary complexity

We live, then, in an intricately ordered world. But beside this lies another wonder: the wonder that a species exists which is able to trace that order. At one level, of course, we are ourselves part of that order, our lives conforming to complex physical, chemical and biological laws; and underlying these lives and these laws is a mind-blowing arrangement of DNA molecules, genes and chromosomes, building up eventually to the greatest wonder of all: the human genome (the complete set of genes).

Scarcely less remarkable than the genome itself, however, is that we (the royal 'We' of collective racial pride) have been able to map it. (The 'We' is important. It is not as if the genome had mapped itself. We are always more than our DNA, and have to insist that it was people, not nucleic acid, who mapped the genome of our species). Not only has God created a cosmos, a thing of beauty and order as distinct from a pile of debris: He has placed within it a creature who, like Himself, is a living intelligence possessed of the curiosity, imagination, powers of observation and mathematical skills which have enabled us to explore and describe the mysteries of light, of the atom, of the microbe and of the outer reaches of space (while learning at the same time that space has no boundaries). It is hard

---

2. John C. Lennox, *God's Undertaker: Has Science Buried God?* (Oxford: Lion, 2009), p. 28.

to decide which is the greater achievement of the divine Word: to create a universe or to form a creature capable of understanding it.

Still, geniuses though we are as compared to the chimpanzee and the ape, our knowledge is always partial. This is obviously true of the individual. The dream of Renaissance Man that he could know all that is knowable has long since been shattered. The language of the modern research microbiologist needs to be translated into 'plain English' before it can be understood by the modern research nuclear physicist and, even if we were to pool all the collective knowledge of the race we would still be faced with mystery. The Unified Field continues to elude us; all our theories leave loose ends; even those of which we are most confident are always open to revision and refutation (just ask Aristotle or Isaac Newton). The principle of *semper reformanda* is as applicable to science as it is to theology. Indeed, it is only by confronting 'modern science' with the organised scepticism of the refereed journals that science can make any advance. And when we add to these limitations the abhorrent uses to which we have so often put our scientific discoveries, we quickly realise that, while we wonder at the intellectual prowess of our species, we must also recognise that we have stamped our depravity on even the greatest scientific achievements. Far from beating our swords into ploughshares, we have beaten our most brilliant insights into weapons of mass destruction. But this takes nothing away from the fact that God, the eternal living Intelligence, has left His footprints on the physical universe; and in one instance, 'Man,' has formed a creature bearing His own image as a living and loving intelligence.

3

✤ HIS FOOTPRINTS IN ✤ CREATION

God has clearly left His footprints on the physical universe, but not only there: He has also left them on the story of the human race. He is not, as Deists suggest, merely a great mechanic who put the Machine together and then left it to run itself. Nor is He an absentee landlord who left the human tenants of His estate to run it (and make a mess of it) without supervision, intervention or accountability. The very nature of God as Life, Love and Logos rules out such an idea of His relationship with the world. After all, the reason He made us was that He might love us, walk with us and keep in touch with us. This is what we mean by divine providence. Not only has God made us: He keeps an eye on us, preserves us and governs us; and this providence applies on both the mega-scale and the micro. It takes in the storms on the face of the sun, the fall of the sparrow and the beauty of the lily. But, above all, it takes in God's personal, active and intimate engagement with the story of humanity.

This engagement began in the Garden of Eden, and though the Fall violently disrupted the relationship, it didn't end it. God kept talking. Indeed, His immediate response to their sin was to speak to them. Of course, the tone had changed. It was admonitory, and even ominous. They had brought a curse on the ground, and yet would remain for ever dependent on it; and to it one day they would return, 'for you are dust, and to dust you shall return' (Gen. 3:19 ESV). But He was still talking to them, and in them to us, and His words were not all doom and gloom. Yes, so long as history lasted there would be enmity between the Seed of the Woman and the Seed of the Serpent, the infernal mastermind behind their sin, but in that struggle her seed would triumph, the human race would be finally redeemed, and for that redemption God Himself would take full responsibility. What is more, from the beginning to the end of that great work He would keep talking, and we would know He was there not only because, like a great artist, He had left behind a sublime portfolio of His work, but because He was still at work; in the course of that work, He kept on explaining it, listening to us and acting for us. From Noah's Ark to the Empty Tomb, and from Adam in the Garden to Saint John on Patmos, His voice was never silent – and it is still not silent.

God's conversation partners

The outstanding example of God's post-Creation activity is His involvement in the history of the people of Israel. How did *they* know that God existed? Was it because they had mastered Anselm and Aquinas and were familiar with the theistic proofs? Surely not! They knew because He had spoken to them and kept on speaking; they knew because He kept on fulfilling His promises and carrying out His threats. Indeed, the key figures in their history had been His intimate conversation-partners. Abraham knew God was there because God had called him, directly and personally; not only had He called him, but He made him a great promise. His descendants would be as numerous as the stars in the sky; they would inherit the earth; they would be a blessing to all nations. To any human ears, including Abraham's own, this was ridiculous. His wife, Sarah, was well past the menopause, and he himself was a hundred years old. But they took God at His word, though not without a struggle – and He kept it. Over the next two thousand years, He maintained a unique relationship with the innumerable descendants of this elderly childless couple, or, to put it more colloquially, He stayed in touch, and through them, He stayed in touch with the whole human race, never allowing them (or us) to forget Him.

This meant three things in particular. Firstly, God was an inescapable presence in their daily lives; secondly, He repeatedly perforated their history in a series of mighty acts, sometimes of deliverance and sometimes of retribution; and thirdly, He chose from among them the great prophets who would deliver His messages to the human race.

The key moment in this history of relations between God and ancient Israel was the Exodus, the event which laid the foundation of the nation's history. After centuries of enslavement in Egypt, Abraham's family, now vastly increased in number, were groaning under the tyranny of a regime bent on genocide. God heard, and God came down (Exod. 3:7, 8). Such language doesn't mean that the author of Exodus subscribed to the idea that God lived a few thousand feet above the earth. Throughout the Bible, such spatial metaphors are used to underline the fact that God is far above us in power, knowledge, wisdom, holiness and sheer splendour; far above our ability to manipulate Him, and far above our capacity to capture His glory in human words or concepts. He is high and lifted up (Isa. 6:1): the *creator* of time and space, not confined by either. But at the same time, His ear is attuned to earth and His eye instantly alert to developments within His creation.

He saw, then, the plight of the Israelites; He heard their cries; He came down and He acted. He raised up a leader, Moses; He divided the Red Sea; He guided His people through the desert; He brought them to the Promised Land. This is the story narrated in Exodus, Numbers and Deuteronomy; and it is narrated not as a national myth, but as a factual history which isn't in the least bit interested in flattering the people whose deliverance it describes. It is not merely 'inspired by real events', like a TV drama-documentary. It is an authentic record of the events themselves, and it is these events which undergird and explain the faith of the nation. They believed in God because they had seen Him act; and considering that we, the Christian nation (1 Pet. 2:9), are also the children of Abraham, we have to embrace the Exodus and the events which followed it as key moments in our own national history. We believe in the LORD, the God of Israel, not on the basis of philosophical arguments, but because of what He did for our fathers, Abraham, Isaac and Jacob.

Engagement with individuals

But although the Exodus stands out as the supreme Old Testament moment of contact between God and humanity, it is by no means unique. Time and again, God acted decisively in history as His people faced the hostility of such great world powers as the Syrians, the Assyrians and the Babylonians. Indeed, the whole of the Old Testament is a reminder that God is not only the Almighty Maker of heaven and earth, and not only one who makes occasional contact with His world, but a solicitous and ever-vigilant Father who stays in constant touch and makes His presence felt, not only in the mega-shifts of world history, but in the lives of individuals.

Fortunately for us, we have well-documented accounts of God's interventions in the lives of key Old Testament personalities. Moses, David, Elijah, Elisha, Isaiah, Jeremiah and Ezekiel are prime examples. All were men of strong faith, but we have to emphasise once again that this faith was not merely the result of an implanted sense of deity or of logical inference from the coherence of the universe and the structures of the human mind. They believed because of what God had done in their lives; what He had done in their lives, He has also done in our lives as members of the Christian nation. We have a collective memory of unforgettable contacts between God and our people.

Intimate conversations

Very often, these contacts were oracular, God speaking majestically from such places as the heights of Sinai or the glory of the *shekinah*. But some key Old Testament figures also enjoyed the privilege of intimate conversations with God: conversations so intimate that God sometimes seems to be speaking to them as His equals. We see this, for example, in Moses. When God calls him, he is not happy and responds with a series of protests, beginning with, 'Who am I?' (Exod. 3:11), followed by, 'I don't know your name', then by, 'They won't listen to me', and culminating in, 'I am not fit to be your spokesman. I am not eloquent.... I am slow of speech and of tongue' (Exod. 4:10 ESV). Through it all, God engages in patient dialogue with a reluctant prophet.

We find the same thing in the account of the call of Jeremiah who, when told of his appointment as a prophet, responds in the same tone as Moses: 'Ah, Lord GOD! Behold, I do not know how to speak, for I am only a youth' (Jer. 1:6 ESV). And, once again, God responds patiently: 'Do not say, "I am only a youth"... Do not be afraid of them, for I am with you' (Jer. 1:7 ESV).

But even more remarkable is the interaction between God, Isaiah and King Hezekiah with regard to the king's illness (2 Kings 20:1-6, Isa. 38:1ff.). To begin with, the prophet is sent with the message, 'Set your house in order. You're going to die. You won't recover.' On the face of things, that seems final, but the king responds by having his own conversation with God, reminding Him how faithfully he had walked before Him and done what was good in His sight. Then, almost immediately, God responds by sending Isaiah with another message: 'I have heard your prayer and seen your tears. Behold, I will heal you and add fifteen years to your life.' On the face of things, this is a remarkable change of direction on God's part, but, looked at more closely, it is a revelation of God as one prepared to act as a real conversation-partner, listening to what the king has to say, and incorporating the king's wishes into the final outcome. We have to remember that it was God's own initial word that prompted the king's response, but the key thing is that, for the purposes of this conversation, God assumes the position of one whose first pronouncement was only provisional and who was thus open to talking about it.

The most remarkable conversation of all, however, is the one between God and Jonah recorded in Jonah 4:1-11. Jonah is angry because, though he had been sent to pronounce doom on Nineveh, God now appears to have changed His mind in response to the city's repentance: Nineveh would not be destroyed after all. This was all very well for the city, and entirely in keeping with God's character as a gracious and merciful God (Jonah 4:2), but, from Jonah's point of view, he had been made to look a complete fool, he had lost the will to live, and so off he went to mope in the shade of a primitive booth he had built for himself. The booth hadn't been very effective, however, and God had kindly raised up a large plant to provide some proper covering.

But then the plant withered and died, leaving Jonah even more distraught and angry. Again, however, God speaks, and this time He focuses on Jonah's inconsistency. Jonah is angry that the plant has been destroyed, and angry that Nineveh, with its huge population, has *not* been destroyed. For the purposes of the conversation, the Creator-creature relationship has been reversed. God has to justify Himself to Jonah. But the really striking thing here is that God and the prophet are sharing the same time and the same space, and that God is presenting Himself as one who, *for the sake of this dialogue*, had known no more than Jonah. Neither the one nor the other appears to have anticipated that the city would repent.

Before we dismiss the portrayal as 'primitive', we should remind ourselves that there is a similar moment in John's account of the ministry of Jesus. Confronted by the need to feed five thousand hungry people, the Lord asks the disciples for advice, but the gospel carefully records that Jesus already knew what He should do (John 6:6). Even so, the question precipitates a real conversation, Jesus learns that there is a young boy in the crowd who has five loaves and two fish, and *acting on this information,* He feeds the multitude.

'They'll never believe you spoke to me!'

One of the protests uttered by Moses in his conversation with the LORD was, 'They will not believe me or listen to my voice' (Exod. 4:1 ESV). The same scepticism still prevails among us today: How can we be sure that such conversations between heaven and earth ever occurred? But Moses, Isaiah, Hezekiah, Jeremiah and Jonah were sure. They were sure, not only because of what they had seen and heard, but because of the sequels. In each conversation, promises were made, and these promises were kept. The LORD *did* deliver Israel from Egypt; Hezekiah's life *was* spared; the many warnings shared with Jeremiah *were* abundantly fulfilled. For such men, of course, God was there 'in the beginning' and it was not from these conversations that their faith took its origin. But their faith found confirmation, and came to a deeper understanding, through their experience of God speaking *to* them and *with* them.

This confirmation did not end with them, however. We share in it because we can claim for ourselves the language of Hebrews 1:1, 'God spoke to *our* fathers by the prophets' (ESV) (italics added). They are our people, part of our Christian history; and taken together with the theophanies of the Old Testament and the post-resurrection appearances of Jesus in the New, they are reminders that even after God drove us out of Eden, He still kept in touch.

But are such conversations not very much a thing of the past: does God no longer keep in touch? Christians know this is not true. For one thing, God is still speaking to us through the prophets and the apostles, whose words, vibrant with life, are the church's most precious possession. But this is not all. In daily prayer, we are still in conversation with God, and He still answers. Granted, the answers are not always luminous, any more than they were for Jonah, and God's being within shouting-distance doesn't mean that He always comes running, or that He always does exactly what we tell Him would be the appropriate course of action. Prayer is not a case of placing an order with Amazon and receiving the goods by Prime Delivery the next day. But it does mean that, time and again, He hears us when we share our fears and pray that what we dread will not materialise; conversely, that when we pray for outcomes that seem to be too good to be true, He delivers precisely such an outcome (Eph. 3:20).

Every Christian life is punctuated by memorable answers to prayer. God gives the grace that keeps us from going to pieces (Heb. 4:16); He heeds our intercessions on behalf of those who are struggling; He braces us for duty, temptation and pain; He 'soothes our sorrows, heals our wounds, and drives away our fears.' When we are weak, He makes us strong. When we preach with poor, lisping stammering tongues, our words become the saving power of God. And every Christian pastor who has seen ordinary men and women triumph over crushing adversity knows that the great promise of Isaiah is as valid today as it was two thousand years ago: those that wait on the Lord still renew their strength, they still mount up with wings like eagles, they still run and are not weary, they still walk and are not faint (Isa. 40:31).

Faith finds confirmation (and self-understanding) in the fact that when it prays to the one it believes in, He still hears and answers.

4

✛ JESUS, GOD AMONG US ✛

From the very beginning, God was actively engaged with humanity, but one moment in this engagement towers above all others. In Jesus Christ, God took our nature, personally entered the history of fallen humanity, and lived a life which, while fully and authentically human, shone with the glory of the divine.

For the present, we can take His humanness for granted. Jesus knew hunger, thirst and weariness; He wept; He washed His students' feet, and from His wounded side there flowed human blood and human fluids. All this the Apostle John, a Jew who would have recoiled with horror from ascribing divinity to any human being, had seen at first hand. Yet, Jew though he was, that is precisely what he saw in Christ: the glory of the divine (John 1:14). This 'man' was the eternal Word who, when time began, was already in being, and had given being to the world and to everything that lived in it (John 1:1-3). Now He had 'become flesh' (John 1:14), uniting Himself to human nature in such a way that in Him God dwelt among us, to be seen and heard and conversed with, and travelled with, and eaten with. Yet, even as He went about doing all these ordinary human things, John saw, shining through His life, a glory that was 'matchless, God-like and divine.'

But can such a faith explain itself? Yes, and the explanation begins by homing in on the single most obvious fact about Jesus Christ. He was utterly unique, and that doesn't mean merely that the portrait handed down to us by His followers is unique, but that the portrait could never have been drawn had not the man Himself been unique. Mere evolution could never have produced Him, nor could the human gene pool; and it is hard to imagine Him as no more than a speck from the fallout of the Big Bang. He joins us and becomes one of us, but He is not 'from here'. He is 'from away,' from the outside, and He comes surrounded by the aura of the supernatural. He has powers and qualities and characteristics that transcend human potential, and by possessing and exercising them He is living proof that behind time and space, there is another order of reality, invisible, eternal and all-powerful. We look at Him and see one 'than which nothing greater can be conceived'. No other man can compare with Him; and no creation of the greatest theological imagination could excel Him. When we see Him, our hearts tell us that, while less could not satisfy, more could not be desired; and so we gladly adopt the adoring words of the Apostle Thomas, the erstwhile doubter, 'My Lord and my God!' (John 20:28).

Extraordinary power

What are those qualities of the historical Christ which are at the same moment so reassuring and so compelling?

First, His extraordinary power. He was not, of course, either the first or the last to work miracles. Moses, by the mere touch of his staff, divided the Red Sea. Elijah brought a widow's son back to life. Elisha cleansed the Syrian general, Naaman, of his leprosy. The apostles Peter, John and Paul performed multiple signs and wonders. But the fact that prophets and apostles possessed such powers poses no threat to the uniqueness of Jesus. At one level, indeed, they serve the same purpose as His, underlining the same fundamental truth that beyond and above 'nature' there is another order which can command obedience from every force in the natural world. From this point of view, Moses, Elijah, Jesus and the apostles have a common ministry. Just as there is continuity between the prophetic message of Jesus and the message of God's Old Testament spokesmen, so His miracles were in complete harmony with those of men like Moses and Elijah; taken together, they were in complete harmony with the fundamental premise, 'In the beginning, God.' The power that created the universe would hardly have had a problem turning water into wine (John 2:5-11).

Yet, just as Jesus' message sheds new and even revolutionary light on the nature and purposes of God, so His miracles have a glory all their own. The difference appears most clearly when we compare them with those performed by His apostles. They, too, healed the sick and even raised the dead, but they did so in *His* name; and whereas Moses, for example, acted only on God's instructions, Jesus acted on His own initiative. He spoke, and it was done, just as in Genesis God spoke 'and it was so'. The storm on the Sea of Tiberias is calmed, the dead Lazarus comes forth, the lame walk, the deaf hear and the blind see; and these are not isolated or occasional instances. They are daily occurrences, spontaneous, effortless and imperious; and they are never mere wonders designed, liked the tricks of the magician, only to impress. They are acts of benevolence, as befits the character of one who is the incarnation of the love and compassion of God. But at the same time, they are reflections of an invisible order capable of modifying the natural world at its will.

Yet, having said that, 'order' is maybe not the right word, because it suggests an impersonal regime, whereas the truth here is supremely personal. The invisible 'order' is none other than God, the eternal living and loving Intelligence who gave the universe birth, but never surrendered control of it; and Jesus acts not merely as one who represents God, but as one who *is* God, though in servant form. It is not His actions alone that evoke wonder. He Himself evokes wonder: 'What sort of man is this, that even winds and sea obey him?' (Matt. 8:27 ᴇsᴠ). We are taken back to the memorable account of a storm at sea in Psalm 107:23-30. The mariners, disoriented and scared out of their wits, cry to God, He hears them, and He calms the storm and hushes the waves of the sea:

> The storm is changed into a calm
> at his command and will;
> So that the waves which raged before,
> now quiet are and still.
>
> (Ps. 107:29, *Scottish Metrical Version*)

It is this same person, this same God, we meet in Jesus Christ. Disease, death, demons, the very deep, do His bidding; and their compliance, recorded in the pages of history, is a standing reminder that 'nature' is neither self-originated nor self-controlling. Just as it is history, not philosophy, that establishes *my* existence, so it is history, not philosophy, that is God's great witness; and it follows from this that the way to establish the faith of our children is not by introducing them to so-called theistic proofs but, as the psalmist reminds us, by telling them the stories that we ourselves heard from our mothers and fathers about the glorious deeds of the Lord and the wonders He performed (Ps. 78:3-4). The proof that 'there is a god' lies in these glorious deeds, not in recondite arguments accessible only to the philosophically literate.

Holiness and purity

But Jesus was not only unique in power; He was also unique in the holiness and purity of His life. Pilate could find no fault in Him (John 18:38), and later critics have fared no better. In fact, it is by the standard that He Himself set that He is judged and, even then, no one has yet been able to suggest any way in which He could have been better. What makes this all the more remarkable is that He lived in the full glare of publicity, and amid all the hustle and bustle of human life. John the Baptist chose the life of a desert solitary, and some of Jesus' later followers have likewise sought refuge from pollution and temptation in the seclusion of monastic life. But Jesus grew up in the despised town of Nazareth and spent the decisive years of His life under the scrutiny of His fellow Galileans, and amid the sins, sighs and sorrows of Jerusalem. He saw the magnificence and ruthlessness of power, He knew the pressures of poverty, He endured the head-turning dangers of adulation and fame, He faced torture and death. Yet He takes no shortcuts, makes no compromises, seeks no revenge and never pleads that He is too busy to help. He fears no man, He sides up to no man, and to this day the challenge He Himself laid down remains unanswered: 'Can any of you prove me guilty of sin?' (John 8:46)

History has seen nothing like it. He breaks the continuum of human selfishness, ambition and earth-bound obsession. He is tested by friend and foe, beset by threats and traps, endures provocation and treachery, encounters humbug and hypocrisy and yet, while no sin is condoned, no sinner is crushed, and no need is ever ignored.

All this can be summed up in 'the sinlessness of Christ', and the phrase is correct as far as it goes. But it is a negative, serving only to tell us what is *not* there. But what of the positive? What are the outstanding features of Jesus' moral and spiritual life?

First, His love of God. It is important to be specific here. Love, vague, ill-defined and autonomous, is the great chant of our age, worshipped almost as a deity in its own right. But it wasn't simply the fact that He loved that made Jesus unique. Fallen humanity is perfectly capable of love. A man can love a woman or love his family or love his country or love his co-religionists or love those who share his ideology and his political programme. But how much evil has been perpetrated in the name of such love! It has served as a cloak for infatuation and lust, bred corruption and murderous jealousy, destroyed families, fostered genocide, condoned flagrant evil, and lit the torch of religious persecution.

In the case of Jesus, however, love was first and foremost love of God; and He loved Him unfailingly, with both the profoundest reverence and the easiest familiarity. He saw God as His Father and Himself as His only Son, but He saw Him, too, as His righteous Father and as His holy Father; and love therefore meant obedience. He loved doing God's will, He gave Him the glory for all the mighty acts of His own ministry, He spoke as God told Him to speak, and He accepted lovingly the 'cup' the Father gave Him to drink, even though He knew that that cup meant all the horrors, physical and spiritual, of the cross. Here, there is utter consecration, a life given over entirely to pleasing God, or, more boldly, to giving God pleasure.

Of course, Jesus is not the only one who has loved God. The saints of the Old Testament loved Him (Ps. 116:1); the apostles loved Him; all Christians love Him. But in all these cases, love stutters and falters. There are periods of disobedience and calamitous disloyalty, and moments of lament and protest. The lives of Moses, David and Peter make this clear, and the biographies of later Christian saints make it clearer still. There are moments of disgrace in the lives of Augustine, Luther and Calvin, but there are none in the life of Jesus, and the only explanation for this is that, though He dwelt among us in flesh and blood, His roots lay elsewhere. His character, no less than His miracles, is supernatural, and proof in itself that the world we see and touch and hear, the world of rigid physical and biological law, is not all. There is another Order, or Person, from which the divine may come to us in human form and dwell among us holy, harmless and undefiled.

The second outstanding feature of Jesus' moral and spiritual life was compassion. He loved His neighbours in all their shapes and forms: family, friend and foe; Jew, Gentile and Samaritan; religious leaders and religious outcasts; resistance-fighters, collaborators and the soldiers of an occupying army; beggars, lepers and the mentally ill; politicians and academics; the immoral and the self-righteous. He is never at a loss. No sin is condoned, and no need is ignored. When tempted to use His extraordinary powers to relieve His own distress, He refuses, but He uses them freely to relieve the distress of others. He heals the sick, He feeds the hungry, He gives the bereft back their dead, and, at the same time, He engages in a ceaseless preaching ministry which boldly challenges the priorities of the culture He lives in, and turns its values upside down. He warns of the dangers of wealth, and pronounces the poor blessed; He demands that we love those who hate us as well as those who love us; He extols meekness, and condemns aspirations to pre-eminence; He disregards the social conventions that governed relations between men and women; He champions the ostracised and rebukes the hypocrisy of those who rush to judge the fallen; He denounces those who exploit widows and orphans, those who defend their inhumanity on the grounds of prior religious commitments, those who take the joy out of religion by adding hundreds of taboos to God's mere *ten* commandments, and those who destabilise marriage and family life by promoting easy divorce.

All this clearly involved enormous personal cost. Day after day, Jesus had to engage in long hours of public teaching, striving to make Himself heard (without public-address systems!) to what were often huge congregations. The crowds pressed upon Him, there were incessant requests for help, and powerful opponents heckled Him and constantly sought to trap Him. He was dogged by both embarrassing adulation and contemptuous rejection. Giving Himself unreservedly, there was little opportunity for privacy or rest: no time or place which He could call His own. When He seeks to withdraw, the crowds find Him and follow Him. He has come to serve and to be available whenever He is needed; and the motives which drive Him are themselves unique. He is not like Gandhi, placing Himself at the disposal of a cause backed by millions, or like a campaigning politician doing whatever it takes to secure election and influence. The lepers and cripples and beggars He helped were in no position to repay Him, and least of all to promote His cause. Apart from one or two exceptions (most notably Mary Magdalene), everyone He helped disappears from the story, having given nothing in return. He helps, simply for the sake of helping, driven only by compassion; and when He is executed there is no surge of outraged sympathy.

Paul's great hymn on love (1 Cor. 13) is now acclaimed by every ideology on the planet, and even those who deplore the Apostle's theology would fain profess that they steer by its compass. In reality, only one man has ever lived it – Jesus Christ. The fact that He did live it, is yet another indication that He was no mere man and no mere fragment of soiled humanity. He alone was untainted by envy and boastfulness, arrogance and rudeness, irritability and resentfulness. He alone did not insist on His own way, but always prioritised the interests of others. Of Him alone could it be said that He bore all things, believed all things, hoped all things and endured all things.

The significance of this must not be lost on us. It means that the uniqueness of Christ does not lie only in His divine identity, fundamental though that is. He is also unique as a man. He is free from all the defects which we take to be part of the very meaning of being human; conversely, He shows a level of philanthropy unparalleled in human history, a philanthropy which sets Him apart and which must be described as simultaneously human and superhuman. He is of us, and yet not of us. He is other than we are, even in the highest reaches of our achievements. He is uncanny, and He is all of these things not only because of the wonders He performed and the flashes of deity which shone through the veil of His humanity, but because of the way He performed being human. No other human biography approaches His. Indeed, every attempt to treat Him as the subject of a normal biography has been a conspicuous failure. Nor has fiction been any more successful. None of its creations rivals, or even approaches, Jesus Christ. At the highest level of its genius, it has been successful in portraying credible, and even compelling malevolent characters such as Iago, Shylock, Lady Macbeth, the Satan of Milton's *Paradise Lost* and Bill Sikes in Dickens's *Oliver Twist*. It has succeeded, too, in portraying dark, volcanic figures such as the Heathcliff of *Wuthering Heights* and psychotics such as Robert Wringham in James Hogg's *Confessions of a Justified Sinner*; flawed heroes such as Othello, Coriolanus and Hamlet; and the trapped, destructive heroin-addicts of Irvine Welsh's dark, yet illuminating novel, *Trainspotting*.

An unflawed hero, but authentically human

But where is the unflawed hero who is, at the same time, authentically human? Hagiography may attempt it, but only at the cost of telling the camera to lie. The greatest saints of Christianity (or any other religion) have all been deeply flawed. Only in the case of Jesus Christ would anyone ever think of proposing a PhD thesis on His sinlessness. In every other instance, from St Francis to Dietrich Bonhoeffer, the fact of the subject's being human would instantly deprive the thesis of all academic plausibility. Yet, in this one instance, it is entirely co-herent, and not simply for *a priori* theological reasons, but because a perfectly sinless life is precisely what the records of His life point to; we can refuse to accept the evidential value of these records only by dismissing them as pious fictions.

But this, too, would come at a price: the price of crediting a random collection of Galilean fishermen with a level of genius far beyond the world's greatest dramatists and novelists. The gospel-writers avail themselves of none of the arts which connect readers to works of fiction. They make no use of the fortunes of romance or the conquests of war or the machinations of court. Their subject has no endearing weaknesses or charming flaws. How can such writings, and such a subject, be remotely interesting? And yet He is, to the extent that millions who never saw Him have fallen in love with Him. That He was, and is, a man, there can be no doubt. He hungers and thirsts and gets exhausted. He is tempted. He has friends and enemies. Born in a stable, He becomes the target of plots at the highest level. He rejoices and He weeps. Yet there is never a lapse. He loves unfailingly, but not wimpishly. A man of strong courage, it almost fails Him in Gethsemane as He faces the real horror of the cup, but He conquers His fear and moves resolutely forward. He warms to sinners, yet never condones sin. He is tender to the fallen, scathing to the censorious. He works wonders, yet never descends to the level of the magician. He preaches long sermons, but peppers them with unforgettable aphorisms. He makes up memorable stories and tells them brilliantly. He outwits those trying to entrap Him. He stands human values on their head. He speaks to God with extraordinary familiarity, and yet with unfailing reverence.

The portrait is unique, and it is unique because there stands behind it a historical figure who was Himself utterly unique. Nature cannot explain Him. His human genome, I suspect, would reveal nothing extraordinary (apart from the absence of any clues as to His human paternity). The idea of a continuous chain-of-being from primate to man could find no appropriate link for Him. Secularism can dismiss Him only by recasting 'The Early Church' as an author of unprecedented genius (though the very existence of this church then becomes a most frustrating puzzle).

Faith, on the other hand, finds its explanation in the most obvious place: 'In the Beginning, God ....' In such a context, Christ is a perfect fit. Without it, neither He (nor anything else) makes any sense.

5

✛ HE IS RISEN ✛

When men crucified Jesus, they thought that would be the last word. Even His disciples thought the same and went home, disconsolate and demoralised. It turned out, however, to be only the word before the last. God would have the last word, the Empty Tomb, and it spoke a great twofold message. It declared God's vindication of His disgraced Son; and it proclaimed, in the most unmistakeable terms, that behind the natural sequence of cause and effect there lies a living, loving and powerful Intelligence who can interrupt and even reverse the sequence at will.

Here again we move, not in the realm of philosophy, but in the realm of history, and specifically in the records of the post-resurrection appearances of Jesus. But before looking at these we should pause over another remarkable appearance: the Transfiguration. There are accounts of it in all three of the Synoptic Gospels (Matt. 17:1-13; Mark 9:2-13; Luke 9:28-36), but the standout account is the personal recollection of the Apostle Peter as recorded in 2 Peter 1:16-18. For him, the story was no fable. He was personally present, as were

James and John, and he saw with his own eyes the transformation in the appearance of the Lord as the glory of the divine, normally veiled by His lowly human condition, shone momentarily in His human form. Never had they seen such brightness, and never had they been more afraid or more disorientated. Not only had they *seen* something extraordinary. They had also *heard* something extraordinary: the voice of God speaking from the Majestic Glory and bearing unforgettable testimony to the honour and excellence of His Son. 'This,' said the Voice, 'is my Son, whom I love. Listen to him!' (Mark 9:7).

We are now separated from this moment by some two thousand years, but Peter wasn't. He was there: he knew what he had seen, and he knew what he had heard, and he was resolved to devote what was left of his life to ensuring that the church would never forget it (2 Pet. 1:15). So sure was he, and so certain, that he would eventually seal his witness with his life.

Here again is history testifying to the extraordinary, and pointing to a glory which was there before ever there was a world; not only so, but a glory which helps us understand how there can be a world at all.

It would have been good, thought Peter, in his very human way, to remain on the mountain where Christ's glory shone so brightly and their own prospects seemed so promising. But they couldn't. Down they had to go, and to a very different world in which the 'beloved Son' would very soon be betrayed, arrested, condemned, crucified and deserted even by God Himself. Good Friday began with Jesus enjoying the Last Supper with the disciples (Mark 14:17). It would end with His burial, cold and lifeless, in a borrowed tomb. The world was rid of Him, the most turbulent of all prophets.

Easter morning

But it wasn't. The women who had followed Him from Galilee had taken careful note of where He was buried, and they waited impatiently for the Sabbath to be over so that they could go and anoint His body (Mark 16:1-8). Their names (Mary Magdalene, Mary the mother of James, and Salome) are carefully recorded, making it easy to falsify their story, had it not been true; their behaviour on Easter morning has the moments of irrationality we might expect in people who have lost a loved one in appalling circumstances and aren't really in control of their own grief. After all, Nicodemus and Joseph of Arimathea had already anointed the body (John 19:39-40), and then there was that huge stone at the mouth of the tomb. They knew they could never move it, but they pressed on regardless.

When they reached the tomb an awesome sight confronted them. Not only had the stone been moved, but, when they entered the burial-place, they saw a figure in white calmly sitting there. It tried to calm their fears: 'You seek Jesus of Nazareth, who was crucified. He has risen; he is not here. See the place where they laid him' (Mark 16:6 ESV). There was nothing there, and never since that day has anyone been able to put anything there. Jesus' tomb remains a void which the best efforts of the Jewish and Roman authorities, sceptical historians and radical biblical scholars have never been able to fill. Contemporary records remain silent, none daring to offer any suggestion as to where it might, after all, be lying. Nor has anyone been able to offer a better account for its disappearance than the one offered by the angel: 'He has risen' (Mark 16:6). And when Mark tells us that the women fled, 'for they were afraid', the emotion is perfectly natural. They had encountered not only the unexpected and the amazing, but the seriously scary and uncanny: the eruption of the divine into human history. And everything in the story fits.

Resurrections aren't proved by voids

But just as wars aren't won by evacuations, resurrections aren't proved by voids. The Empty Tomb was followed by a series of appearances of the risen Christ. We have no reason to think that any of those to whom He appeared was a victim of wishful thinking. Not one of Jesus' followers expected ever to see Him again. Nor were the appearances confined to particular types of individual, or groups, or locations. He was seen by a remarkably diverse range of people: Mary Magdalene; Peter and John; the Eleven all gathered together; the two disconsolate disciples on the road to Emmaus; James, Jesus' brother, who had once thought Him mad (Mark 3:21); and Thomas, who refused point-blank to believe the story (John 20:25). On one occasion, He was seen by a gathering of 500 people, many of whom, according to St Paul, were still living when he wrote his First Epistle to the Corinthians (1 Cor. 15:6). Had the case been subjected to a judicial review, it would have taken many, many months to hear the testimonies, cross-examine the witnesses and listen to the hostile testimony of expert psychiatrists arguing that each of the 500-plus eyewitnesses was as mad as a March hare.

Clearly, the personalities of those privileged to see the risen Christ varied widely, but there is no evidence whatever that any of them was neurotic or delusional; and certainly no evidence that these appearances turned them into incoherent fanatics. On the contrary, they went on to produce the world's most enduring and widely-read literature. Few today could give the names of the great Roman writers of the first century. Livy and Ovid are remembered only by scholars: millions are familiar with Matthew, Peter and John, all of whom saw the risen Christ and went on to write letters and histories which have challenged the world's finest minds for centuries. Besides, they were prepared not only to tell what they had seen, but to suffer and die for it: and that, not only because they knew it to be true, but because they believed that the one they had seen was the very one they would have to meet again on the Day of Judgment.

But no less remarkable than the variety of personalities to whom Christ appeared is the variety of circumstances. He appeared to Mary Magdalene in the very garden in which He had been buried (and in such a lowly form that she mistook Him for the gardener). That same evening, He overtook two men walking home to Emmaus: men who had clearly looked to Him as the Messiah, and whose hopes had been cruelly dashed by the crucifixion. They had a memorable conversation with Him, but as they were about to share a meal with Him, He suddenly vanished. Only then did they realise who the stranger was, and they couldn't wait to tell the news. They immediately retraced their footsteps and made the seven-mile journey back to Jerusalem, only to discover that the disciples already knew; as the excited group discussed the news, Jesus Himself suddenly stood among them, even though the doors were locked.

Thomas wasn't present on that occasion, and when told the story, he dismissed it instantly, declaring that unless he could see and feel for himself the marks of the nails in Jesus' body, he would never believe. A week later, Jesus again appears to the disciples, still meeting behind closed doors. This time Thomas is present, and Jesus offers him the visible, physical proof he had laid down as a condition of believing. Ashamed of his doubts, Thomas can only exclaim, 'My Lord and my God!' (John 20:27).

John tells of another, remarkably leisurely occasion, when, early one morning, Jesus revealed Himself to a group of disciples by the Sea of Galilee (John 21:1-14). They were fishing, and He stood on the shore, unrecognised. He approached them and asked if they had any fish. 'No!' They had caught nothing. He told them to change their tactics and to cast their nets on the other side of the boat. They took a huge haul, and only then did they recognise that it was the Lord. By the time they got back to land, He had already prepared a barbecue, and they enjoyed a hearty breakfast.

It is remarkable that the Gospel of John, which begins with a sublime proclamation of Christ as the eternal Word of God (John 1:1-17), should end with this, the most physical of all the New Testament accounts of the resurrection.

On this occasion Jesus spent considerable time with the disciples, and it is clear from the opening chapter of Acts that this was not unusual. In the forty days between His resurrection and His ascension, He resumed His teaching ministry, patiently clarifying what He had earlier taught about the kingdom of God, commissioning them as His witnesses, making plain the universal range of their mission, promising that they would shortly be empowered for this mission by the Holy Spirit, and directing them to remain in Jerusalem till that promise was fulfilled (Acts 1:1-9). There is nothing rushed here: His lessons even left time for questions (and sometimes not very apt ones, Acts 1:6-8).

The series of resurrection appearances ends with the Ascension of Jesus, recorded in Luke 24:50-53 and Acts 1:9-11. Gathered at Bethany, the disciples receive Jesus' final benediction and stand transfixed, gazing heavenwards till a cloud (the symbol of the divine presence) takes Him out of their sight. But whereas the women on Easter morning had fled from the tomb, traumatised, the disciples on this occasion returned to Jerusalem with great joy (Luke 24:52). Yet the Ascension was a defining moment. They would never see Him again in this life, and though His future disciples would love Him, they would love Him as those who had never seen Him (1 Pet. 1:8).

The Damascus Road

But there was one clear exception: Saul of Tarsus, to whom Jesus appeared on the Damascus Road (Acts 9:1-19). He himself describes this appearance as 'untimely' (1 Cor. 15:8, ESV), and this was probably one of the reasons why many members of the church in Corinth regarded him as a second-rate apostle. He himself is clear, however, that what happened to him was not some mere visionary experience. It was an actual appearance of the risen Christ, who quickly identified Himself as 'Jesus' (Acts 9:5). Saul had seen the Lord, as surely as Peter and James and John had seen Him.

This was the origin of Paul's faith in Christ. Up to this point, the persecution of the church had been his profession, the extinction of Christianity his consuming passion. Jesus was a fake, a fraud and a blasphemer, and yet His movement was gathering momentum at such a rate that He was now, in Saul's view, a threat to both his religion and his nation. There is no sign here of any predisposition to believe that this man, this Jesus, whom God had so clearly cursed, might have risen from the dead; no sign of self-doubt; no hint that Saul's attitude had begun to change and that he had begun to think that perhaps the rumours about Jesus were true. There was certainly nothing in Judaism, nor in the other religions of his day, to prompt him towards believing that a crucified man had risen from the dead.

Never did Paul's enmity against Christianity burn more intensely than it did on that journey to Damascus, his mind filled with thoughts of hatred and slaughter. But then came a spiritual thunderclap. In the full flush of fanaticism, he is arrested by the one he knew was dead. A light from heaven falls on him and he falls to the ground confused and blinded. A Voice speaks. It knows who he is, and it knows his mission: 'Saul, Saul why are you persecuting me?' 'Who are you, Lord?' he cries. 'I am Jesus, the one you are persecuting.'

Saul of Tarsus is an historical figure and, as such, proof once again that God is to be found not at the conclusion of elaborate philosophical arguments, but within the history of redemption. His faith rested on what he had seen with his eyes and heard with his ears. Yet his experience on the Damascus Road was not only an *historical* event. It was also an *historic* one, on which the whole subsequent human story would turn, as Saul travelled the known world preaching, writing, organising, and carrying the extraordinary message of a crucified and risen Messiah to regions which still lay in the grip of paganism and polytheism. It is a thrilling story, but its roots lie in this encounter with a dead man who had risen. The one he hated, he now loved; the one he had seen as the enemy of his people was now their Messiah; the one from whom he had recoiled as a blasphemer was now God's beloved Son, vindicated in the wonder of His resurrection.

From this point onwards, Saul of Tarsus would live for Christ. For Him, he sacrificed his academic and political career. For His sake, he would face flogging, shipwreck, privation, contempt, imprisonment and, finally, execution. For Him, he would use his mighty intellect. For Him, he would do whatever it took to make people listen to His gospel.

Why so much space to the resurrection?

Why devote so many paragraphs to the resurrection? Not simply to prove the resurrection itself, but to use it to point to something even greater: the existence of a living, loving, intelligent and powerful God, the Father of our Lord Jesus Christ, who can make the dead live and who, as the great guarantor of Moral Order, will one day put everything right. Sometimes that moral order seems to be completely overthrown, as it did when lawlessness crucified Christ. But God raised Him from the dead, and by doing so, He gave history an entirely new colour. Light reigns.

6

✟ THE BIBLE ✟

There remains one further mighty act which helps faith to understand itself: the Bible. It is a miracle in its own right.

It is not, however, the sort of miracle claimed for the Qur'an by Muslims, who believe that the very words of the Qur'an existed from all eternity, that Mohammed received them from an angel, memorised them, and then recited them to companions who in turn recited them to others. No human mind was involved in the composition at any stage.

The Bible, by contrast, is a miracle that God achieved through human authorship, a point which St Peter makes with remarkable emphasis when, referring to the prophets, he writes (to quote him literally), 'spoke from God *men*' (2 Pet. 1:21, italics added). It is more a library than a single book, composed over hundreds of years by a remarkably varied succession of men, each writing in his own style, each reflecting his own temperament and each betraying his own personal flaws. Moses is not David, Isaiah is not Jeremiah, and St Luke is not St John. Some were literary geniuses, most were not. Some were men of profound intellect, some were not. Almost every one has his moments of self-doubt and near-despair, and each falls at some point or other below the standards he preaches.

Nor is it only the authors who reflect widely varying personalities. Precisely because the writers and their cultural settings are different, their compositions embrace many different kinds of literature. There are great historical narratives such as the story of the Exodus, the gospel accounts of the life of Christ, and the record of the growth of the early church which we find in the Book of Acts. There is great poetry, not only in the Psalms, but also in the lyrical passages which sometimes arrest us even in the middle of long sections of prose (for example, 1 Corinthians 13). There are proverbs and parables and even fables (Judg. 9:8-15). There is the enigmatic Book of Job, recording one believer's anguished protests against the ways of the Almighty. There is the wisdom of Ecclesiastes, telling us to view life from its Ending. There are mundane instructions about war, husbandry and hygiene. And there are the sublime theological flights of John's Prologue and Paul's Epistle to the Ephesians.

On some rare occasions, the biblical authors are writing to divine dictation: indeed, in the case of the Decalogue, the commandments are written by God Himself on tablets of stone, and precise details for the construction of the Tabernacle and for the Levitical rituals are also handed down directly by God. But these are exceptions. The norm was that the biblical writers had to endure all the travails common to human authorship. They used the language of their own time and place, they laboured over word selection, and over the links by which they would move from one topic to another. They drew on existing sources, oral and written, but selected them carefully and edited them judiciously. They drew on concepts such as covenant and adoption which were current in the society of their day, and even drew occasionally on the writings of pagan poets. On the other hand, they avoided words like *eros*, the common word for romantic love, because it was open to serious misunderstanding and might convey an entirely false idea of God's love. And all the time, whether writing the Book of Genesis or the Epistle to the Galatians, they remain focused on the needs of their original readers and on the pastoral challenges facing the church of their own day. Every book of the Bible was addressed to a specific contemporary situation.

Nor are the differences between the biblical writers limited to matters of personality, style and genre. There are also differences in the theological colouring. Each era and each writer makes their own distinctive contribution, as God reveals Himself not all at once, and not in monochrome, but 'line upon line', teaching each generation as it was able to bear, and building on what readers already knew.

This is exactly what we are told in the opening words of the Epistle to the Hebrews: the Scriptures were given at various times and in diverse ways. Sometimes, there were long hiatuses, as in the period between Malachi and John the Baptist, while at other times (such as the age of Moses and the era of the apostles) there is a flood of sacred writings. But no later age simply reproduces the message of those which have gone before. Instead, as the sacred writings accumulate and the library is expanded, there is steady progress towards fuller and deeper revelation. The clearest example of this, obviously, is the contrast between the Old Testament and the New. Psalmists and prophets foretold the Advent and the Cross with remarkable clarity, considering that they wrote almost a thousand years before the event, but, compared to the apostles, the light they shed on the life and work of the Messiah shines but dimly; very often, it is only the light of the New Testament that enables us to see the light shining in the Old.

Yet even within the same eras, each writer has his own concerns and introduces his own concepts: Isaiah with his Servant Songs, Jeremiah with his message of the New Covenant, David wrestling with the lows and highs of personal religion: personal sin on the one hand, the mercy of God on the other. The same pattern occurs in the New Testament, though over a much shorter timescale. Overarching all is the unique ministry of Jesus, distinguished from all others by His Messianic consciousness and His assurance of His own divine identity, but also distinguished by such features as His use of brilliant parables, memorable one-liners, and His habitual reference to Himself as 'the Son of Man' (a title never applied to Him by any of His followers).

The writings of the apostles are, of course, entirely derivative from the teaching of Jesus, and all of them follow the pattern set by John the Baptist when he diverted attention from himself to Christ (John 1:20). But even as they bore their witness, they were painfully conscious that they knew only in part. Even though they spoke in words taught by the Holy Spirit (1 Cor. 2:13), the message transcended both their powers of conception and their powers of expression, forcing them to speak of riches which were 'unsearchable' and a joy which was 'unspeakable'.

But still, each is making his own unique contribution. Matthew alone gives an extensive summary of the Sermon on the Mount, while John alone speaks of Christ as the Logos. To Paul, we owe not only the clearest revelation of the doctrine of justification, but also the description of the incarnation as a self-emptying (*kenosis*) on the part of the pre-existent Christ (Phil. 2:7). To the writer to the Hebrews, we owe the description of Christ as a priest, fulfilling the symbolism of the Mosaic sacrifices; and to the Revelation of St John, we owe not only the visions of apocalypse and cataclysm, but the unforgettable image of the slaughtered Lamb standing in the centre of the Throne (Rev. 5:6).

Speaking for God

No doubt about it, then: the Holy Scriptures reflect on every page a vibrant yet humble humanity, conscious of its servant-role. But amid all this humanity and all this humility we encounter an amazing claim. It was already made by Moses, and it got him into deep trouble. He claimed that God had spoken to him and appointed him His spokesman. He spoke for God. Time and again the claim provoked bitter anger. Even his brother, Aaron, and his sister, Miriam, resented it: 'Has the Lord indeed spoken only through Moses? Has he not spoken through us also?' (Num. 12:2 ESV). But the same claim pervades the ministry of later prophets, who regularly preface their messages with the words, 'Thus says the Lord'; and although many modern biblical scholars dismiss the claim out of hand, Jesus endorsed it unreservedly. 'Scripture,' He said, 'cannot be broken' (John 10.35 ESV). It is of inviolable authority, and it is so because its every word comes from the mouth of God (Matt. 4:4). His apostles took exactly the same view.

But before we look at the apostles' attitude to Scripture, let's pause for a moment over Jesus' attitude to His own words. He clearly saw them as absolutely authoritative. One clear example of this is the language He used in the Sermon on the Mount when laying down His famous series of 'antitheses' to the revered rabbinical tradition. 'You have heard,' He declared, 'But I tell you ...' (Matt. 5:21-48); and what He went on to tell them was that their traditions amounted to nothing less than a dilution and evasion of divine law. God, He declared, forbids hate as well as murder, and lust as well as adultery; God commands love for enemies as well as for friends; God commands that, instead of demanding an eye for an eye and a tooth for a tooth, we should turn the other cheek.

The language is uncompromising, and it never dates. Jesus is assuming and asserting His authority to pronounce judgment on the most revered of human insights and traditions, and He underlines this by His dramatic conclusion to the Sermon. Just as a house built on sand will never stand against flood or storm, so a life which ignores His words will be swept away (Matt. 7:26-27).

It goes without saying that the apostles accepted unquestioningly the divine authority of Jesus. Paul, for example, preaches only what he has received from the Lord (1 Cor. 11:23-25; 15:3; Gal. 1:11-12). But like Jesus Himself (and like every pious Jew of their day), the apostles cherished without reservation the belief that Scripture is the Word of God. In their case, of course, 'Scripture' meant the Old Testament, and their deference to its authority is clear throughout their writings. True, it is no longer their only authority. The words of the Lord are still remembered and have begun to circulate in both oral and written form (Luke 1:1-2); along with the writings of the apostles, these words (preserved for all time in the gospels) would soon be regarded as of equal authority with the Law and the Prophets. Indeed, we already find Peter equating the writings of 'our beloved brother Paul' with the 'other Scriptures' (2 Pet. 3:16 ESV).

This didn't mean that the writings of the Old Testament were now obsolete. Jesus had already made plain that He had not come to abolish the Law and the Prophets, but to fulfil and clarify them (Matt. 5:17), and this is why it was precisely to the Old Testament writings that the apostles turned for illustration of their beliefs and for proof of their doctrines (see, for example, Paul's argument for his doctrine of justification in Romans 4:1-12). It is also why the Book of Psalms still remains the supreme inspiration of Christian praise and prayer.

But although the canon which the church inherited, the Old Testament, was not abandoned, it was augmented by the gradual addition of what Christians now know as the New Testament; and this was no mere supplement, merely fine-tuning the earlier revelation. The history of redemption had moved forward, and it had moved forward dramatically. Not only had the Messiah come: He had come as God incarnate. He had died to atone for the sins of the world; He had poured forth His Spirit to empower His people; He had created a New Israel, embracing all nations (Matt. 28:19); one day, He would return in power and glory.

This was new, radically new, and, just like the Exodus, this new divine act of redemption had to be illuminated by a new divine act of revelation. Indeed, this new revelation, to be given through the apostles, was itself a redemptive act, as indispensable as the cross itself.[1] Without it, the world could never have been saved. There had to be a *word* of the cross (1 Cor. 1:18), as well as the *fact* of the cross, only God could provide it, and the apostles would be His chosen spokesmen.

But while they delivered this revelation through both their preaching and their writings, they continued to reflect on the nature

---

1. For the same reason, Christ had to be a prophet, as well as a priest and a king.

of the Old Testament and, by implication, on the meaning of 'sacred scripture' as such. Their mature views on the subject are recorded in two memorable passages: 2 Peter 1:20-21 and 2 Timothy 3:16-17.

Peter's statement, as we have seen, clearly emphasised that the Scriptures were written by men, but it also makes clear that, though they wrote and spoke as men, what they said was no mere reflection of their own human analysis of events or of their own insight or foresight. On the contrary, they wrote as men who were carried by the Holy Spirit: not only prompted or led, but carried. They said exactly what the Spirit intended them to say.

This view of the Old Testament was fully endorsed by St Paul: 'All Scripture is breathed out by God' (2 Tim. 3:16 ESV). In the previous verse he has referred to the Scriptures as 'the sacred writings'. This immediately means that we cannot accept the view, now so dominant in the field of Biblical Studies, that we are to treat the Bible as we would any ordinary book. Apart from all else, few ordinary books go about proclaiming that they have been breathed out by God. If the claim is false, we should throw the book away. If it's true, then the reader is on hallowed ground. The Scriptures are, indeed, 'writings,' but to the Apostle Paul they are sacred or holy writings, and totally different in character from all other human literature.

What makes the Scriptures sacred?

But what, precisely, makes them sacred? The fact, declares the Apostle, that they are 'breathed out' by God. The word Paul uses here is *theopneustos*, and older versions took it to mean that the Scriptures were 'inspired' by God, which suggests that God produced the Scriptures by 'breathing into' the men who wrote them. But the real idea is quite different. *Theopneustos* means literally 'God-breathed', and what Paul is speaking of is not 'breathing *into*' but 'breathing *out*.' The Scriptures were breathed out by God; this refers to all Scripture; and it refers to them precisely as writings. The point is not that the men who wrote our Bible were inspired, but that their writings have this unique quality that they are the breath of God. In other words, whatever is Scripture is the Word of God.

Paul doesn't venture to give any explanation of the nature of this out-breathing; neither does any other biblical writer. We are told that the writers were carried, but not how; and we are told that their writings were breathed out, but not how. What we do know is that, whatever the nature of the divine action, it did not preclude human action or suppress or bypass the personalities of the biblical writers.

Occasionally, indeed, like a manager dictating to his secretary, God told the writers exactly what to say. Sometimes, He revealed Himself to them in theophanies or in various mighty acts like the Exodus and 'carried' them as they described what they had seen. Sometimes, He provided for several different people to witness the same event (the cross, for example), but gave each of them the freedom to express in his own way what he had seen.

And sometimes, as in the case of the Psalms and the Apostolic epistles, God speaks through the outpourings of the writer's own soul. For example, as Paul writes his Epistle to the Romans, he is hearing no voice and seeing no vision, or in any objective sense engaging in conversation with the divine. Instead, he is thinking, and through *his* thinking, God speaks.

To what extent Paul was, what the Puritans called, a 'painful' (painstaking!) author, we shall never know. It would be fascinating to see his original manuscript and check whether he ever scored out a word to replace it with another, more precise or more elegant. Probably not! Paul writes with passion, and sometimes pours forth his thought in a torrent, careless of grammar and too busy to revise. But when the resulting product, *The Epistle to the Romans*, is ready, God is prepared to endorse this letter, written to one church with its own set of problems, as *His* letter to the whole church, and to the church of all ages. And what is true of *Romans* is true of the whole Bible. God, in the language of modern copyright, has identified Himself as the author.

7

✣ A BOOK LIKE NO OTHER ✣

What I have in the Bible, then, is a book of dual authorship, human and divine and, if asked what we mean by the inspiration of Scripture, all we can say is that it is that mysterious divine action by which God secured that the human word we read in the Bible is also in its entirety His Word. In recognition of this, I am called to believe that whatever it says is true. That is the essential nature of faith.

But can such a faith give a coherent account of itself? Is it supported by the understanding? Or, in other words, if God is one than whom a greater cannot be conceived, is the Bible also a book than which a greater cannot be conceived?

This cannot be a matter of merely showing that the Bible is free from error or that it is not at variance with science or that its writers were accredited by the miracles they produced or that they had the gift of foretelling great events long before they happened. It cannot even be a matter of the accuracy of the picture the Bible draws of human nature. Both history and fiction bear equally eloquent testimony to the depravity of 'Man'.

Where faith in Scripture finds its coherence is in the fact that the Bible conforms to what we would expect of a divine revelation. It resonates with the sense of divinity which exists in every human heart. It stimulates the seed of religion sown by God Himself in every soul. It presents a God before whom we can fall in both self-abasement and humble adoration. It is a balm to the wounded soul.

All this resolves itself into one great unifying fact: the glory of Scripture is that it is the bearer of Jesus Christ, and in Him faith sees a form of the heavenly with which it is entirely satisfied. At faith's lowest ebb, and when we see others forsaking Him in droves, we say, 'To whom shall we go? You have the words of eternal life' (John 6:68). If Christ is not there, if Christ is not God, and if God is not Christ, we care for no other. For us, He has spoiled every other deity. But when faith is in full sail, it looks at Him and sings with joy; and we prize the Sacred Scriptures precisely because they bring us Christ and disclose, in and through Him, such a knowledge of God as could come only from heaven itself. The portrait as it stands is matchless and beyond the creative imagination of even the greatest human genius. If we could not worship *Him*, we should have to worship the artist; but then, in this case the artist, too, is divine. The portrait of the divine Son has been drawn for us by the divine Father, who alone knows Him (Matt. 11:27).

The portrait of the divine Son

What are the features of the portrait that faith finds so reassuring?

First, that in it we see God as one prepared to take our human nature and to share our human experience. As a mere idea this would have been beyond both Judaism and Islam: so abhorrent that it would never have occurred to any Jew or Muslim to invent it. But in Jesus, it becomes a reality. He became flesh, taking our nature in the low condition in which we have had to exist ever since the Fall. He wasn't merely a Spirit-filled man. He was the eternal Son of God, yet He was that Son in servant-form, uniting Himself to humanity so completely that He had a human body and a human mind and lived, here on earth, a totally authentic human life. He had human ancestors; He was a member of a human family; He had (and needed) human friends and He lived out His days surrounded by all the sins and sorrows of first-century Palestine. He experienced what it was like not to know (Mark 13:32), and what it was like to fear death, and even to taste it (Heb. 2:9). It meant that He learned what it was like to be dependent and vulnerable, and to have to live by prayer. It meant that the Son of God came where He would be despised, rejected, mocked, spat upon and cursed. It meant His having to face at least one moment (in Gethsemane) which almost broke His mind (Matt. 26:38). It meant becoming a victim of towering injustice: being betrayed, arrested, flogged, crucified. It meant that men would have to arrange for His funeral, and women would grieve at His passing.

Yet, truly and perfectly human though He was, He was never a mere man. Prior to His human birth, writes the Apostle Paul (Phil. 2:6), Christ Jesus already existed in the very 'form' of deity but, moved by a divine altruism, He renounced His right to come into this world in glorious heavenly majesty and came, instead, in servant-form, humbling Himself so far as to hang upon a cross, anonymous, His glory veiled, alone, powerless and contemptible: looking for all the world like a wasted life. This is nothing less than God Himself moving towards a whole new range of experiences, and these are now part of the history of God. In Christ, the eternal, living, loving Intelligence who created the heavens and the earth has had personal experience of human weakness.

Secondly, in and through Christ we see that, while God is one, He is not solitary, eternally alone, unloved, and without relationships. As we read the story of Jesus' life, listen to His discourses and overhear His prayers, we learn that the eternal Father has an eternal, uncreated Son, sharing His nature and equal to Him in power and glory; and a Holy Spirit, also eternal, and also sharing fully in the divine glory. This mystery, the Trinitarian nature of God, is revealed at the very beginning of Jesus' life when, courtesy of the gospels, we have the privilege of being witnesses of His baptism. The Three are here: the Son is baptised, the Spirit comes upon Him, and the Father's voice proudly acknowledges Him as His beloved Son.

Then, in the Prologue to John's Gospel, we read that at the heart of deity there is with-ness (or, as it is called today, relatedness). In the Beginning, the Logos, who would one day become flesh, was already *with* God: God with God. Yet, at the same time, Jesus can declare, 'I and the Father are one' (John 10:30): distinct, yet one, with a unity that far transcends any unity that can exist between individual human beings. As one, they act together to design, create and preserve the world; as one, they communicate, not like us, through words but through an intimacy such that each fully knows the others' mind; as one, the Three are utterly, perfectly happy in each other's love. They adore each other, glorify each other and are perfectly fulfilled in each other. The divine has no need that is not met in this fulness of affectionate relationships. Had there never been man, universe or angel, the eternal Trinity would have been a perfect community of love.

The three great 'religions of the Book,' Judaism, Christianity and Islam, all agree that the world owes its origin to one eternal personal Creator, but both Judaism and Islam recoil with abhorrence from the doctrine of the Trinity: Jews because it seems to contradict their bedrock belief that God is one; Muslims because they cannot separate the idea of God having a Son from the idea of His having had sexual relations with the Virgin Mary. Even to many Christians, the doctrine of the Trinity seems more of a burden and a conundrum than an asset.

It is certainly a mystery, and, from our human point of view, counter-intuitive. But mystery is inseparable from deity. A God from whom our intellects could expel every element of the mysterious would be no God at all. The God of Christian faith certainly cannot be contained within our human creeds and concepts, and even less can He be tidied up by our human words.

The business of theology, it has often been said, is not to solve puzzles, but to identify mysteries. Sometimes, however, the mystery sheds light on a puzzle, and here is a case in point. Far from being only an embarrassing conundrum, the doctrine of the Trinity illuminates one of the most central messages of the Christian faith: 'God is love.' He never became love, nor did His love ever have a beginning. 'Vast as eternity Thy love,' sang Isaac Watts. God was always love, and within the communion of the Father, the Son and the Holy Spirit, He always enjoyed love. But if there was no Trinity, if there was no Father, Son and Holy Spirit, no unity of coeternal and coequal persons, then God would have been in the same position as Adam before the creation of Eve, and a sympathetic observer, had there been one, might well have commented, 'It is not good for God to be alone.' He would have been a monad surrounded by nothing. But if, in God, there was always Another, and always with-ness, and always relatedness, then faith can understand how God can be love, and how that love can express itself in a benevolence that wants to communicate His own happiness to beings of another order: beings whose happiness was the aim God had in mind when He created the world.

And if the Son is one of the eternal Three, then we can understand how, even as He lives a normal human life, He is the revelation of deity. He is His revelation because He *is* God, albeit, in Him, God has accommodated His glory to the weakness of our human eyes. Likewise, since He is God, then the compassion that shines through His servant-life is the compassion of God; and by the same token, when the Holy Spirit comes to live in us, it is God Himself who comes. The life of God is in the Christian soul.[1]

---

1. For an exposition of this, see Henry Scougal, *The Life of God in the Soul of Man*, first printed in 1677 and often reprinted since.

Thirdly, in and through the Christ of the Bible we meet a God who not only took to Himself our human nature but also took upon Himself our human sin. This was the core of John the Baptist's witness to Jesus: 'Behold, the Lamb of God, who takes away the sin of the world!' (John 1:29 ESV). What is remarkable here is that the Apostle John began his gospel by setting Christ forth as the eternal divine Logos and now, a few verses later, he sets forth this divine Logos as the great sin-bearer, to be sacrificed as an atonement for the sins of the whole world. God answering for our sin! God judged in our place! God carrying our sins in His own body to the cross (1 Pet. 2:24). God being made sin for us (2 Cor. 5: 21).

Sin: an immediate turn-off

Why is the very mention of such an idea an immediate turn-off? The answer is simple: it involves the notion of sin, it is now a sin to mention the word sin, and even when we do mention it, we immediately take the nastiness out of it. Everyone sins, we say; or, our sins are mere peccadilloes, common human infirmities; and in any case, it's God's job to forgive them. Sometimes, even less seriously, it's what the church is there for: to give absolution. Not long ago I heard an Army Chaplain tell of a day when the battalion, just returned from a vigorous day's training, was being debriefed by its Commanding Officer. He concluded by ordering the Chaplain to come forward: 'Come, Padre, and forgive us our sins.'

Many will think such a light-hearted view of sin splendidly modern. In reality, it is as old as time, and it was exactly this attitude that prompted Anselm in the eleventh century to write his classic book on the Atonement, *Cur Deus Homo?* ('Why Did God Become Man?')[2] The book is in the form of a dialogue, and at one point, Anselm's conversation-partner, Boso, suggested that sin might be cancelled by a single act of repentance; to which Anselm replied,

---

2.   See Anselm of Canterbury, *The Major Works*, pp. 260-356.

'You haven't yet reckoned with the gravity of sin.'[3] Boso's words summed up the mediaeval attitude to sin, and they sum up, no less accurately, the modern one; and precisely because we don't take sin seriously, we have no patience with the idea of atonement, or with a God who makes a fuss about it.

Yet, at the same time, the ideas of accountability and retribution lie at the very foundation of modern society. This is why, all over the world, the victims of crime, oppression, and negligence cry out for justice, and clap and cheer when a jury finds an accused person guilty. This is why we take with the utmost seriousness any breach of our own civil and criminal laws, and any violation of our own human rights. And this is why we have our justice systems and our police forces and our prisons. The very fact that such arrangements exist in all nations and in all cultures points to the ineradicable human belief that breaches of the law deserve retribution.

But what we guard so jealously in connection with human laws and human governments, we deny to God, even to the extent that we refuse to recognise His Court; and this leaves human justice hanging in the air. If there is no ultimate justice, by what star are our legislators to steer? And if they don't have the sanction of the supreme and universal judge, by what right do our petty magistrates dare to deprive a man of his liberty, and in some countries even of their life? Judicial retribution derives its legitimacy only from God, who will one day call each one of us (including our judicial systems) to account.

When that day comes, will any of us be able to plead our innocence? The divine law is clear: 'You will love the Lord your God with all your heart, and you will love your neighbour as yourself.' Every single one of us has violated it, and we have compounded our violations by brazenly assuming that the first part of it has now been repealed. We rightly recognise the gravity of such crimes as sectarian hatred and racial hatred and insist that they be punished

---

3.   *Ibid*, p. 305.

with the full rigour of the law. But God-hatred, we assume, carries no serious consequences: in fact, it's really, really woke.

And so it will remain till the day we meet the Supreme Judge face-to-face. It's easy to put the thought of that moment out of our minds. Yet it can never be entirely eradicated. The Stoic faced it, and steeled himself to die 'as without hope, so without fear.' The tormented MacBeth faced it and cried, 'Will all great Neptune's oceans wash this blood clean from my hands?' (*Macbeth*, Act 2, Scene 2). Hamlet faced it, and declared, 'conscience does make cowards of us all.' If only he could be sure that death would bring oblivion! But 'the dread of something after death'

> puzzles the will,
> And makes us rather bear those ills we have
> Than fly to others that we know not of.
>
> *Hamlet*, Act 3, Scene 1

This is why human history bears such eloquent testimony to our desperate attempts to appease an angry deity. We have sacrificed countless millions of sheep, goats, lambs and even children; we have done penances, performed rituals, gone on pilgrimages, endured vigils, fasts and self-flagellation; we have renounced the world and disappeared into deserts; we have sold all that we had and given it to feed the poor ... and still our consciences have not found peace.

But then, into that ancient Graeco-Roman world of countless temples and fierce deities, came the Gospel of Jesus Christ to announce that God doesn't demand that we personally make atonement for our own sins, and doesn't insist that we can come to Him only if we are bearing gifts. This is the great, core Gospel idea. We don't have to earn forgiveness: it is rich and free. In a way, that is all that need be said; that is where faith and repentance begin. The Prodigal can return home just as he is.

But it is not all that *can* be said. There is more: God is right to forgive sin, not because it doesn't matter, but because His Son took the guilt of humanity upon Himself; and in language chosen by God Himself, He became the Lamb who bears, and bears away, the sin of the world. In the name of humanity, and by agreement with His Father, He offered to God the sacrifice of a perfect obedience. In the name of humanity, He bore the judgment our sin deserved. In the name of humanity, and from within its depths, from within its very heart, He so lived and so died as to satisfy God that it was right to forgive sin; and no sinner who comes seeking forgiveness in the name of this Man will ever be turned away (John 6:37). He is the Way to God (John 14:6).

But one Man did this? Yes, one man, in one time, and in one place, but a man whose life and death had universal significance, because He was no mere man but the eternal Son of God, who had taken man's nature and man's place and man's liabilities. In Him, the God-Man, God Himself, the Father, the Son and the Holy Spirit, bore the full cost of redemption so that if we ask, 'Is atonement necessary before God can forgive sin?' the answer has to be, 'No, not for you. The Son of God has done it all. For you, grace is rich and free.'

But isn't such a forgiveness merely external, leaving our hearts still unchanged and our lives still self-centred and ungodly? No again! Because here, we meet yet another reason for the apostolic superlatives. Christ, by His life and death, has secured not only that our sins be forgiven, but that the Spirit of God should come, take up residence in our hearts and transform us from the inside. Not only did Christ die for us; by His Spirit, He lives in us, and this life of God in our soul bears the fruit summarised so splendidly in Galatians 5:22-23. The forgiven life is marked by love, joy, peace, patience, kindness, goodness, faithfulness, gentleness and self-control.

The final outcome

But it's not only the depth and the cost of God's love that confirms our faith in Him as the one than which a greater cannot be conceived. There is another wonder: the final outcome that God had in view.

He wanted His creatures to have eternal life. This takes us back to where we started, and particularly to the point that 'in the Beginning was life.' Before there was sun or moon, man or angel, time or space, there was life: life that had no origin, because it was eternal. The nature of that life we have already seen. It was the life of the eternal Trinity, a life of shared love and unqualified blessedness, and for us to have eternal life means to share in this very life that God had from all eternity.

This takes us to the very limit of our superlatives and to the borders of the incredible. The life of the Eternal was a life of perfect blessedness; or, to give it its full emotional impact, it was a life of perfect happiness. What God wishes for us, and what Christ secured for us, is that we should share in this, the happiness of the divine; share in the love of the Father, the Son and the Holy Spirit; share God's delight in His creation; share in the Father's adoration of His Son.

We come back once again to the question, Why did God create the world? The traditional Christian answer, as we have seen, has been that He created it for His own glory, and that will always remain an important truth. But it should not be the last word, because it suggests that the glory of God depends on His creatures, and that He created the world so that it would sing His praises, as if otherwise, His praise would go unsung. But the deeper truth is that He created the world for His own satisfaction, and when it was finished, He looked, and it was 'very good' (Gen. 1:31). He was delighted. It made Him happy. It gave Him pleasure; and if that was the purpose of creation it was also the purpose of redemption; or, echoing the words of Isaiah 53:11 (KJV), after the travail of His soul He was satisfied. His whole plan of salvation was motivated by love, and this meant God doing His very best for the world, and particularly for His church. It meant that, from the very beginning, His intended outcome was to present us faultless in the presence of His glory with exceeding joy (Jude 24). It meant that, not in our doxologies only, but in our happiness, God takes pleasure; and to that end, He will keep giving Himself to us throughout all eternity. It is in the joy of His creation that God is glorified.

But let's remind ourselves how we got here or, more precisely, why we got here. The point of this brief summary of the doctrine of redemption was not so much to explain and defend it, but to underline the unique nature of the Book that bears such a message: a message than which a greater cannot be conceived, and which is communicated to us through a book than which a greater cannot be conceived. The Bible itself is one of God's mighty acts, a key moment in the great succession of redemptive events such as the Exodus, the Incarnation and the Resurrection. It is a visible, tactile miracle which, with gathering clarity and fullness from Genesis to Revelation, tells of a God and of a love such as the human imagination could never have conceived. It is an enduring divine footprint on the landscape of creation, and it says, 'God was here.'

8

✢ 'I BELIEVE': FAITH AND ✢ CERTAINTY

So far we've looked at *what* we believe. But what do I mean when I say, with the Apostles' Creed, 'I believe'?

First and foremost, belief is a matter of the mind. It means being persuaded that something is true and that we believe it as a matter of personal conviction and certainty. In John 11.27, for example, we hear Martha declaring, 'I believe that you are Christ, the Son of God' (ESV). That is the most fundamental of Christian beliefs, but around it there cluster several others, and they can all be expressed under the simple form of words, 'I believe that ....' For example, 'I believe that Christ was born of the Virgin Mary; that He was crucified under Pontius Pilate; that He rose again the third day; and that He will one day return to judge the living and the dead.' I also believe that God is willing to forgive my sins and that one day my body will rise again. If we lose these beliefs, or sit loose to them, we lose Christianity itself.

Behind such belief lay *knowledge*, and specifically the knowledge conveyed through the preaching of the gospel. The Athenians might worship the Unknown God (Acts 17:23); a Christian cannot. How, asks the Apostle Paul, can anyone believe in a God of whom they have never heard; and how can they hear without a preacher? (Rom. 10:14) The fact that Christ was the Saviour of the world was not a dictum of common sense, and neither was it an insight available through the prevailing philosophies of the age, Stoicism and Epicureanism. Nor again was it a shared belief of all the world's religions. Men and women could get to it only through hearing God's Good News about what His Son had done for the salvation of the world (Rom. 1:1-3). But though it was God's story, it could be told only through human heralds and messengers who would pass on from person to person and from house to house the news that God had made peace with the world through Christ (2 Cor. 5:19). Only through knowledge of this message could people come to faith in Christ two thousand years ago; only through this knowledge can they come to it today, and only through this knowledge can faith be nourished and stimulated.

To the early Christians, faith was a matter of deep certainty. 'Faith,' declares the Writer to the Hebrews, 'is the *assurance* of things hoped for, the *conviction* of things not seen' (Heb. 11:1 ESV, italics added). G. K. Chesterton once observed that, 'what we suffer from today is humility in the wrong place. Modesty has moved from the organ of ambition [and] settled on the organ of conviction; where it was never meant to be. A man was meant to be doubtful about himself, but undoubting about the truth; this has been exactly reversed.'[1]

Such an accusation could certainly not be brought against the Old Testament saints whose endurance and exploits are recorded in Hebrews 11, and neither could it be brought against the first Christians. They were weak in themselves, but strong in faith, certain that Christ had died for their sins, risen from the dead, and taken His place as Lord of all. This is why thousands of them were

---

1. G. K. Chesterton, *Orthodoxy* (1908. Reprinted London: Fontana, 1961), p. 31.

prepared to suffer martyrdom rather than renounce or deny their beliefs. They were sure that behind the visible world there lay an unseen one; certain that God by His mere word had created the universe; and certain that God would deliver on all His promises about the future. To faith, these promises had such solidity and substance that believers could already 'see', albeit at a distance, the city whose builder and maker was God (Heb. 11:10).

Faith is certain, then, that God exists, that He speaks through the prophets and the apostles, and that, one day, He will regenerate the universe and create a new heaven and a new earth (Rev. 21:1). Such certainty was already under suspicion a hundred years ago, as Chesterton reminded us. Today, it is derided. It is not only that people disagree with what we believe. They deplore certainty itself. Doubt, as Herman Bavinck once remarked, has become the sickness of our time.[2]

There are two main reasons for this: first, the philosophical assumptions that govern the thinking even of those to whom the name Socrates suggests only a Brazilian footballer; secondly, the sceptical historical scholarship, promoted even within the church itself, that has undermined confidence in the trustworthiness of the Bible.

Philosophical assumptions

First, the philosophical assumptions. We live in a climate of wide-ranging scepticism, where not only philosophers, but the man and woman on the street happily accept the idea that there is no such thing as 'truth.' Instead, truth is seen as something subjective and personal, reflected in such comment as, 'It's true, if it's true for you;' or, more cynically, 'One person's opinion is as good as another's.'

There are certainly many subjects which must always remain matters of personal opinion, especially in such areas as politics,

---

2. Herman Bavinck, *The Certainty of Faith* (1901. Republished Potschefstroom: Institute for Reformational Studies, 1998), p. 1.

art, literary criticism, the heroes and villains of the past and, not least, controverted points of theology. But in real life, few people believe that their personal convictions are truths only for them. This is certainly not the opinion of the LGBT 'community', who demand that their views be protected by statute; or of Muslims, sensitive to the merest hint of Islamophobia; or of those who march under the banner of 'Black Lives Matter'. Such groups do not regard their opinions as merely private beliefs. They see them as universal truths demanding the assent of all reasonable human beings.

But in one area, religion, certainty is excluded (with, it must be said, great certainty) and relativism has taken a firm hold: so much so that most theologians have now decided that their business is no longer the pursuit of truth, or the study of God, but only the study of what other theologians have said about God. To claim to have even a tenuous grasp of the truth is dismissed as arrogance.

This relativism has its roots in the philosophy of Immanuel Kant (1724–1804), and particularly in his distinction between faith and knowledge. Certain things, Kant argued, are matters of knowledge, others are matters only of faith; and among those which are matters only of faith are the soul, life after death and, above all, God.

This distinction itself, however, rested on a further distinction between what Kant called the *phenomena* and what he called the *noumena*. The *phenomena* referred to the sensible and material world, consisting of things we can see and weigh and measure. This world could be investigated by the scientific method, which involved not only the use of reason but also the use of our senses, and yielded empirical or experimental certainty. Here there could be real knowledge.

There could be no knowledge, however, of the unseen world, the *noumena*. We could form ideas of God and of life after death, and we could have opinions on them, and we could have *faith* in them. But we could have no *knowledge* of them.

It is important to remember here where Kant was coming from. He was reacting to a widespread rationalism which thought that it could know the Almighty (the *noumenon*) unto perfection. Kant rightly disputed this, and here, his thinking is entirely in line with Christian faith, which insists that the human mind can never have more than a partial knowledge of God. He was also right when, in a major publication, he argued that there could be no religion within the limits of reason alone.[3] Religion required certainty, and pure reason, unable to attain to any real knowledge of the *noumenon*, could never provide that.

But, true though it is that we cannot know the Almighty unto perfection, it is equally true that neither pure reason nor the scientific method can give us an exhaustive and definitive knowledge of the material universe. Our knowledge of the *phenomena*, no less than of the *noumena*, is always going to be limited and provisional. The visible world may yield many of its secrets to the naked eye, and even more to radio telescopes, electronic microscopes, and proton accelerators, but nevertheless, what we see is only the appearance, not the inner reality.

In Kant's day, neither the gene nor the atom had yet yielded their secrets. What secrets do the phenomena still hold? Beyond number! But they will disclose them only slowly, and sometimes only with extreme reluctance. Every puzzle solved in physics discloses yet another mystery. And the certainty of the scientific community has more than once been misplaced.

This has not always preserved science from hubris. In 1900 Lord Kelvin, renowned as the formulator of the Second Law of Thermodynamics and the concept of Absolute Zero, declared before the British Association for the Advancement of Science, 'There is nothing new to be discovered in physics now. All that remains

---

3. Immanuel Kant, *Religion within the Limits of Reason Alone* (1793, English translation 1934. Republished New York: Harper and Row, 1960).

is more and more precise measurement.[4] A mere five years later, Einstein not only formulated his Theory of Special Relativity, but also laid the foundation for Quantum Theory by demonstrating that light moved, not in a continuous wave but in multiples ('quanta') of tiny particles (later called photons). Together, writes Einstein's biographer, these discoveries 'lit a flame that would consume classical physics'.[5]

Yet towards the end of his life, and after quantum mechanics had gained universal acceptance among physicists, Einstein himself lamented, 'All these fifty years of pondering have not brought me any closer to answering the question, "What are light quanta?"'[6]

The Christian church may well echo this sentiment, and declare that all these thousands of years of pondering have not brought us any closer to a definitive answer to the question, 'What is God?' At the same time, however, we should be thankful for what we do know; and we know because, while unaided human reason is not able to give us a knowledge of the Invisible, the Invisible is able to reveal Himself, and through such revelation to share with us His knowledge of Himself.[7] It is on this fact of divine revelation that all religion rests; above all, it is on this that Christianity rests. The knowledge we gain from such a revelation will, of course, always be partial for the simple reason that the finite lacks the capacity for the infinite; and there are 'secret things,' which might be within our capacity, but which God has kept to Himself. Nevertheless, this revelation yields real knowledge, not only of propositions about God, but of God as He is in Himself.

There is nothing in Kant's thinking to rule out the possibility of such a revelation. He spoke only of the limits of pure reason, and

---

4.   Quoted in Walter Isaacson, *Einstein: His Life and Universe* (London: Simon and Schuster, 2007), p. 90.

5.   *Ibid*, p. 99.

6.   *Ibid*, p. 101.

7.   At this point Scripture endorses the principle that 'only like can know like.' See 1 Corinthians 2:11 ESV, 'No one comprehends the thoughts of God except the Spirit of God.'

God has not left us at the mercy of pure reason. He has shown Himself, entered our human experience, and given us empirical proof, not only of His existence, but of His ongoing relationship with the world and of His concern for humanity. The Invisible gave Himself visibility; the *noumenon* made Himself a *phenomenon*. This is what we have already noted as the experience of Abraham, Moses, David, and the great Seers of Israel. God met them, God walked with them, God held conversations with them.

Above all, this is what we see in Jesus Christ, God incarnate. Time and again the Apostles emphasise His visibility. 'We have seen his glory,' wrote St John (John 1:14); 'we were eye-witnesses of his majesty,' wrote St Peter (2 Pet. 1:16); 'that which we have seen and heard we proclaim also to you,' writes St John again (1 John 1:3 ESV). In Him, God entered time and space, spoke with mortals, altered the course of nature before their very eyes, and personally commissioned them to pass on the news of what they had seen and heard. They did so, and this means that for Christianity the existence of God is not a matter of philosophical or theoretical argument, but a matter of empirical evidence. We believe in a God who speaks and who acts.

This doesn't mean that we place theology in a safehouse beyond the reach of reason. Reason has its own place, because we receive revelation as rational adults made in God's image. Were it otherwise, we could not even begin to understand revelation. But whatever the importance of reason when it comes to interpreting revelation, we cannot allow philosophy to rule out revelation, and neither can we allow reason to subject God's self-unveiling to its own censorship.

It is from this revelation that faith derives its certainty. It is sure that God has spoken, and no less sure that when He speaks, He must be believed and obeyed.

Faith and historical scepticism

The second great challenge to Christian certainty has been the growth of radical historical criticism, especially of the gospels. The eighteenth-century Enlightenment was a protest against authority, especially that of Pope, Creed and Holy Books; out of this arose a determination to treat the Scriptures as you would any ordinary human literature; and, once placed on this platform, Biblical Criticism, particularly of the gospels, became a search for contradictions, inconsistencies and errors, which, it was alleged, undermined their reliability as witnesses to the life and teaching of Jesus.[8]

Such scepticism, circulating within the church itself, clearly had serious implications for Christianity, because it is not, like Marxism or Existentialism, a mere collection of ideas generated by human reason, but news: and if it is fake news, it loses all credit. St Paul put it perfectly: 'If Christ has not been raised then our preaching is in vain and your faith in vain' (1 Cor. 15:14 ESV); and, he adds, we preachers are telling a pack of lies. Every Christian doctrine, from the atonement to the resurrection of the body, falls if the history falls.

One of the most radically sceptical voices, coming this time from the twentieth century, has been that of Rudolf Bultmann. Widely acclaimed as one of the great New Testament scholars of his time, Bultmann was nevertheless prepared to state categorically, 'We can now know almost nothing concerning the life and personality of Jesus, since the early Christian sources show no interest in either, are moreover fragmentary and often legendary; and other sources about Jesus do not exist.'[9]

The first response to this must be that a factual account of the life and personality of Jesus is exactly what the gospel-writers thought

---

8. This does not mean that the academic discipline of Biblical Criticism is itself illegitimate, or that 'critic' in this context should be taken as a derogatory term referring to scholars committed to 'criticising' the Bible. The true goal of Biblical Criticism is to come to an informed judgment on the range of textual, literary, historical, and exegetical questions which inevitably arise in the course of studying the Bible.

9. Rudolf Bultmann, *Jesus and the Word* (1926. English translation, London: Fontana, 1958), p. 14.

they were giving;[10] and even a cursory reading of these accounts provides enough information to furnish a perfectly coherent answer to the question, 'What was He like?' But if they don't give us a factual account, what then do the gospels give? Bultmann's answer is that they give us facts overlaid with, and encrusted in, mythology. But there are huge difficulties in such a construction.

For one thing, there is the scale of the myth the Evangelists are supposed to have created. It is not a myth about a great warrior or a myth about the founder of a great nation or a myth about the adventures of one or other of the gods of Olympus. Nor is it a myth created to be the bearer of some great moral ideal or some aspect of the human tragedy. It is unique among myths: a 'myth' about the one eternal God humbling Himself by taking human nature, living a fully authentic human life at the bottom of the social scale, and letting Himself be spat upon, crucified and buried. It is a 'myth' about a carpenter who spoke as no man ever spoke, and whose Sermon on the Mount was pronounced 'the last word in ethics' by no less an agnostic than Winston Churchill.[11] It is a 'myth' about a man whom the winds and the seas obeyed (Mark 4:41), was witnessed raising the dead, and was Himself raised from the dead. It is a 'myth' that didn't fit into the worldview of Greek or Roman, with their 'gods many, and lords many' (I Cor. 8:5 KJV); or into the worldview of the Jews with their intolerance of any rival to their own Almighty God, Yahweh. How on earth did the early Christians manage to sell such a myth?

---

10.   See, for example, Luke's introduction to his gospel, where he makes plain that his concern is to compile an orderly account of the things reported by those who from the beginning had been eyewitnesses of Jesus' life and ministry. He also describes himself as one who had been 'following things closely for some time past.' He presents himself as neither a theologian nor a creative historian, but as a chronicler albeit from a clear standpoint of Christian faith. 'Impartial' historians will, of course, have their own faith-standpoint, generally one of scepticism towards the claims of the gospels.

11.   Andrew Roberts, *Churchill: Walking with Destiny* (London: Allen Lane, 2018), p. 932.

Secondly, there is the speed with which the myth was formed and established. Within twenty years of His death, Jesus Christ was being publicly worshipped not only in Judaea and Syria, but as far afield as Turkey and Greece. Thirty years after His death, His followers at Rome had become so numerous that the Emperor, Nero, could make them scapegoats for the great fire that devastated the city. At that date, many were still living who had known Jesus as boy and man, had heard Him preach, knew the blind He was alleged to have healed and the dead He was alleged to have brought back to life. Such people could have stopped the 'myth' in its tracks – but they didn't.

Thirdly, there are the men who created the myth. They must have been literary geniuses. But we know who they were; and they weren't. They were men of whom the most that can be said is that they were ordinary: not men of learning, or men of affairs, or men who by themselves could have commanded a following. Two were provincial fishermen, one was an exciseman, and one was a physician who gave up his practice to accompany the Apostle Paul on his missionary journeys. Another was Jesus' cousin, John, whose mother was Jesus' auntie. Yet another was His very own brother, James, who had seen Him grow up and had thought Him mad. It's doubtful if any of them would have known how to start an essay, yet they handed down a story which has lost none of its freshness after two thousand years.

Then there is the form in which their testimony is cast. Here, we are clearly dealing with what Kant would have had to call a 'phenomenon': objects that we can see and handle and read. And what remarkable objects these gospels are! It is not simply the remarkable scope of the narrative they relate, tracing the life of their subject back not only to His infancy, but to His pre-existence in a timeless eternity, and following it through its triumphs and trials to His coronation as the Lord of heaven and earth (and of the mighty Caesar).

The individual component parts of the story are no less remarkable. Which of these Galilean followers of Jesus composed the Sermon on the Mount? Which wrote the Lord's Prayer? Who thought up the parables of the Good Samaritan and the Prodigal Son? Whose imagination conjured up the drama of the storm on the Sea of Galilee? Who created the story of Gethsemane, portraying their Master on His knees mentally as well as physically; or of the cross which seems to move to a climax in the Cry of Dereliction only to be overtaken by the serenity of, 'Abba, into your hands I commit my spirit'? And was it Peter or John or some other fisherman who crafted that artless gem which we know as Mark's report of Easter morning (Mark 16:1-8)?

When historical scepticism comes to grips with the gospels, it is thus faced with two miracles: the invention of the news, on the one hand, and the reporting of it on the other.

9

✢ THE FLIGHT FROM ✢ DOCTRINE

Christian faith has to survive in a hostile world, and very often, as in the persecutions under the Roman Emperor, Diocletian, and the Soviet Premier, Nikita Khrushchev, that hostility has taken the form of murderous violence. But even at times when the church enjoys respite from persecution, the hostility continues, especially in the form of a relentless intellectual attack on Christian beliefs. The philosophers of Athens derided the idea that a man could rise from the dead (Acts 17:32), sixteenth-century Socinianism mounted a sustained attack on the divinity of Christ, eighteenth-century Deism denied the need for any special divine revelation, and, in our own contemporary world, the gospel has to exist in a toxic atmosphere of dogmatic uncertainty and historical scepticism.

Life, not doctrine

Faced with such hostility, it is tempting for Christians to flee to some place where they can feel secure from intellectual attacks, and one such refuge is the plea that Christianity is not about historical facts and theological doctrines, but about a way of life. 'Forget the dogmas,' people say, 'let's just live the ethic of Jesus. What matters is not Christian beliefs, but Christian values.'

Nor is the sentiment confined to those who would happily describe themselves as 'simple believers'. It has also been invoked by generations of distinguished Christian scholars as they struggle to commend the faith to its cultured despisers. The doctrines, they think, are a liability. The Liberal theologian, Adolph Harnack (1851–1930), even suggested that theology has often served only to destroy religion, Christology as laid down in the ancient creeds should therefore be dispensed with, and attachment to Christ redefined as simply keeping His commandments, especially the commandment to love.[1]

Such, from the late eighteenth century onwards, had been the teaching provided in many European theological seminaries, and from these, it quickly spread to Protestant pulpits. It placed Christianity where Kant's critique of theology couldn't touch it, but at a price. All its great doctrines were silenced because, allegedly, they showed Christianity in a poor light. Poets, artists, philosophers and scientists found them repugnant, but if you limited yourself to preaching Christian values, and asked no more of men and women than that they should follow the example of Jesus, that would not only avoid all offence: it would make Christianity palatable to the educated and cultured members of society.

This wasn't a case of mingling a little water with the wine, though that can be disastrous enough. It was a case of throwing out the wine, and offering nothing but water.

A betrayal

But whether at the level of popular piety or of sophisticated Liberalism, the proposal to suppress Christian doctrine and rewrite

---

1. Adolph Harnack, *What Is Christianity?* (trans. Thomas Bailey Saunders, 3rd edition, London: Williams and Norgate, 1904).

Christianity as first and foremost 'a way of life' (in effect a way of 'being good') is a complete betrayal of both Christ and His apostles. Indeed, it is reminiscent of the situation that St Paul describes in his very last epistle, when he warns young Timothy that 'the time is coming when people will not endure sound teaching, but having itching ears they will accumulate for themselves teachers to suit their own passions' (2 Tim. 4:3 ESV); and far from advising Timothy to accommodate this new fashion, he counsels him to 'reprove, rebuke, and exhort, with complete patience and *teaching*' (2 Tim. 4:2 ESV, italics added).

The Lord Himself was a teacher, and was often addressed as such, either under the title *didaskalos* or the title 'Rabbi'; and He could hardly have been a teacher without having some doctrines to teach. His understanding of God as 'Our Father' was a doctrine; His understanding of the cross as a ransom for sinners (Mark 10:45) was a doctrine; and His insistence on the necessity of the new birth (John 3:7) was a doctrine.

And the apostles, too, were teachers. St Paul, for example, describes himself as 'a teacher of the Gentiles in faith and truth' (I Tim. 2:7 ESV. Cf 2 Tim. 1:11), and he crams his epistles with so much doctrine that they've kept theologians busy (and scratching their heads) for two thousand years. Elders had to be 'able to teach' (I Tim. 3:2), 'the faith' itself was a body of truth which could be expressed in 'a form of sound words' (2 Tim. 1:13 ESV), and it had to be guarded as a sacred deposit (2 Tim. 1:12, 4:7). As for the idea that we should forget Christology (the doctrine of the person of Christ) and just get on with living the Christian life, the apostles would have found it both absurd and abhorrent. The great distinction of Christianity was not that it imitated Jesus, but that it worshipped Him, and this worship rested on the most fundamental of all Christian doctrines, the deity of Christ. If that doctrine is not true, worship of Christ is idolatry. If it is true, every knee must bow, including those of His cultured despisers.

Every key aspect of Christianity is similarly founded on doctrine. It is through a doctrine, justification by faith, that we have peace with God (Rom. 5:1). It is the doctrine of Christ's victory over Satan that takes away the fear of death (Heb. 2:15). It is the doctrine of the Second Advent that gives us hope for ourselves and the world. And it is Christology, and Christology alone, that can enable us to live a Christ-like life in this present world, as appears clearly in Paul's invocation of the self-emptying of Christ in Philippians 2:5-11. The Philippians, he writes, should give up their preoccupation with their own individual rights and remember instead the mindset of Jesus. He, eternally existing in the form of God, really was Somebody, but He made himself a nobody, veiling His identity and His glory under the form of a servant. The duty laid down is elementary; the theology invoked to reinforce it is massive. But take away the doctrine of the Lord's eternal pre-existence and the ethical imperative vanishes.

Clearly, then, the early church did not share the anti-intellectualism characteristic of modern Christianity. When Luke, for example, wrote his gospel, he was clearly addressing people's minds, aiming to give his readers certainty with regard to the things they had been taught (Luke 1:4); the Apostle John wanted to confirm his readers in their belief that Jesus was the Messiah (John 20:30); St Peter calls upon us to prepare our minds for action (1 Pet. 1:13); and St Paul speaks repeatedly of the importance of renewal of the mind (e.g., Rom. 12:2, Col. 3:10).

All this was reflected in the way the apostles set about evangelising the world. They saw their mission as a battle for the mind. Only that way could they win hearts. They had to convince a generation stubbornly committed to their own ethnic religions that a crucified Jew had risen from the dead and that He was the Saviour of the world; and while such a message had its own emotional impact, their primary task was not to move people's feelings, but to persuade people that the news was true. The message, 'Live like

Christ,' would follow; but it could only follow. First of all they had to convince men of the facts.

We today are engaged in the same battle, and in a religious context not all that different from the first century. When Dr Billy Graham came to Scotland seventy years ago, he could make assumptions we can no longer make. He was preaching in a Christian country where few, even among non-churchgoers, questioned the authority of the Bible, the resurrection of Christ, or the certainty of judgment to come. Our situation is far different. The convictions and certainties on which Billy Graham built are no longer there, even in the church. Instead, the Christian worldview which once shaped the life of Western Europe, has been replaced by another radically secular one, which, if it thinks of Christianity at all, thinks of it only as owing the world an apology; and which views churches not as live places of worship, but as museums to be visited for their architecture. We no longer hold people's minds. Instead, we are starting from scratch in a world where there are gods many and lords many, and our God is seen only as a spent one.

What is the way forward, then? Let's read Paul's Second Letter to Timothy, and then let's shake ourselves and do what it says: Preach the truth; preach the great doctrines; inform, argue, persuade. And when we feel discouraged, let's remember the Advocate who through our 'poor, lisping, stammering tongues' can persuade the jury that Christ is a great Saviour.

The rigour of Jesus' ethic

But apart from the fact that forgetting the 'dogmas' and just getting on with living the Christian ethic is a betrayal of apostolic Christianity, it also seriously underestimates the rigour of the ethic that Jesus preached, as if living the life were far easier than believing the doctrines. This is far from being the case. In fact, the gospel is precisely for those who have failed dismally to live the life.

Jesus' ethic is summarised for us in the Sermon on the Mount, and when we first approach it, we probably expect to hear Jesus relaxing the stringent standards of the Pharisees and laying down for His followers a yoke that is much easier to bear. But we are quickly disillusioned: 'I tell you, unless your righteousness *exceeds* that of the scribes and Pharisees, you will never enter the kingdom of heaven' (Matt. 5.20 ESV, italics added). In fact, this was already clear from the very beginning of the Sermon, when Jesus delineated the character of the person whom God blesses. It is most peculiar, because the picture He draws is not that of the typical modern good neighbour or even the typical modern churchgoer. Indeed, this blessed person seems at first sight to be dull to the point of morbidity. He is poor in spirit, he mourns, he is meek, and he is all these things because he has faced one great fact: the truth about himself. That is where 'living the Christian life' must always begin. The blessed man or woman is aware of their own spiritual poverty and grieved by it. They are meek because what they know about themselves makes it impossible for them to feel superior to others, and they are merciful because they know that they themselves owe everything to divine grace.

Nor is this all. This person whom God blesses, and who lives the Christian ethic, is pure in heart. His desires and ambitions are pure, and the motives behind them are pure. He hungers and thirsts for righteousness, and the only reward he craves is to see God (Matt. 5:8). The picture immediately takes us beyond ethics into the realm of another-worldly piety, and at first sight it is easy to profess admiration for it. But by nature men don't admire it, and that is precisely why the person who attempts to live the ethic of Jesus, far from being applauded, is going to be reviled and persecuted (Matt. 5:11). We can't escape the contempt of religion's cultured despisers by being the Blessed Man or Woman of the Sermon on the Mount. We can win their respect only by accommodating our ethic to theirs, and by then we have left Jesus' definition of the Blessed Man far behind.

When we come to the Great Antitheses (Matt. 5:21-48), where Jesus contrasts what He expects from His disciples with conventional human ethics, things get even tougher. The tone is set in the recurring formula, 'It is said, but I say to you,' followed by a series of paradigms in which Jesus makes plain just how rigorous and how inward are the laws of His kingdom. Lust as well as adultery is sinful, hatred as well as murder, covetousness as well as theft. Divorce is ruled out, retaliation is forbidden, and, above all, the enemy is to be loved as well as the friend. And so it goes on. Everyone who offends us or discriminates against us, is to be forgiven; we are to renounce the pursuit of earthly treasure; we are to give up being judgmental; we are never to worry about what to wear, or how we look; and we should be on the alert for false prophets because their heresies (their errors in doctrine) pose a mortal danger to men's souls (Matt. 5:15).

The Sermon was never meant to be a checklist. Instead, it cuts to the quick. But even as a checklist, who can tick all the boxes and say, 'I may have no patience with these church doctrines and dogmas, but I live the ethic of Jesus?' In reality, such an appeal is pure legalism, as if we could stand before God and declare, 'I want to be judged by my life and work, and specifically by my compliance with your Sermon on the Mount.' It is a bold claim, even a foolhardy one, and there are two things we need to bear in mind: first, the sermon has in view those who are already disciples; secondly, before we ask to be judged by it, we should remind ourselves that failure has serious consequences.

A sermon for disciples

First, the sermon was addressed specifically to disciples: people who had already enrolled in Christ's school and become citizens of His kingdom. This carries with it a whole cluster of theological implications. The person who is expected to live this sermon is a disciple: someone who has been born again, whose life is driven by gratitude to the God who forgave his sins, and whose overriding concern is that God should be revered and His name hallowed (Matt. 6:9). For such people, to live is Christ. They are united to Christ; Christ lives in them, and because they have this special relationship with Him, they have an equally special relationship with His Holy Spirit, who dwells in them and gives their lives its distinctively Christian character.

We cannot turn round and say, 'I don't want to hear about such theological stuff. I just want to live the Christian life.' Unless we have experienced this 'theological stuff,' we cannot live the Christian life, because that life begins with gratitude for the 'wondrous cross, on which the Prince of Glory died.' Only when we survey that cross (and that means giving it more than a casual glance) are we moved to exclaim:

> Love so amazing, so divine
> Demands my soul, my life, my all.

That's what living the Christian life means: giving God our all, in response to what *He* did for *us* on the cross of Calvary. We cannot despise the cross, or dismiss the doctrine of the atonement as offensive and immoral (as so many professing Christians do), and yet go on to live out the Christian ethic. Apart from all else, we wouldn't have the motivation.

Yet it is precisely the disciple, the blessed man, who is most painfully aware of his failure to fulfil the Sermon. He takes with total seriousness the words of Matthew 7:21, where Jesus declares that only those who *do* the will of His Father will enter the kingdom; and in this context the 'will of the Father' can refer only to the life-pattern described in the Sermon which is now moving to its conclusion. The Sermon is the 'narrow way' that leads to life, and no cry of, 'Grace, not law!' can be allowed to obscure this. The gratitude that fills the heart of a Christian breeds a determination to bear himself in a such a way that his life brings glory to our Father in heaven (Matt. 5:16). Yet, so often, he fails, and he knows he fails;

and then, because he is a disciple, the effect of the Sermon is to drive him to the Cross, the place of forgiveness, where he meets, of all things, a doctrine: 'the blood of Jesus his Son cleanses us from all sin' (I John 1:7 ESV).

Even so, the disciple cannot simply shrug off his failure or take shelter under the fact that every Christian life is haunted by the presence of indwelling sin. That is only part of the picture. The other part is that a Christian is driven by what the Shorter Catechism (Answer 87) calls 'a full purpose of, and endeavour after, new obedience.' He or she is no longer content with their old levels of obedience. Driven by new motives, and drawing on new resources, they resolve on a new obedience; and just how strong the Lord expects that resolve to be is made plain in the uncompromising words of Matthew 5:29-30: 'If your right eye causes you to sin, tear it out ... if your right hand causes you to sin, cut it off.' Sin must be starved of its oxygen.

The cost of failure

Secondly, before we ask to be judged by the Sermon on the Mount, we should ponder the cost of failure. It is spelled out clearly at the end of the sermon itself in the memorable comparison between the man who built his house on the rock and the man who built his house on the sand. Both had heard the sermon and both, we can be sure, had applauded it. They both agreed that mercy was a great quality and so, too, was not being a Pharisee. Indeed, everything in it might well be admired. But still, before you could walk the Way you first of all had to go through a strait gate, where you had to part with so much of your baggage; and the Way itself, the preacher said, was narrow and lonely, and could even get you into trouble. Besides, it very much sounded as if the pursuit of treasure in heaven could severely jeopardise your prospects of even a little treasure on earth. And surely there were exceptions to the Way laid down by the preacher? Am I expected to love *every* enemy?

Must I always turn the other cheek? Must I forgive even those who never said, 'Sorry'?

Clearly, living the Sermon isn't as easy as either the legalist or the liberal thinks. Indeed, implies the Lord, it is easier to prophesy and to cast out demons, than to live the Sermon (Matt. 7:22), and yet, if we do no more than listen and admire, or even listen and resolve, then we are building on sand, and the life we build will be swept away in the flood of divine judgment (Matt. 7:24-27).

And here we come across a remarkable thing: the Sermon makes huge theological claims. Jesus is not, after all, just the simple preacher of the Golden Rule.[2] He is the Judge who on 'that day' will assign to every human being their eternal destiny (Matt. 7:21-23). Of course, we should have read the signs of this earlier on, especially when Jesus calmly, and on His own sole authority, set aside the revered traditions of the ancients and declared, 'But *I* say to you.' Yet here, in Matthew 7:23, the authority He claims is explicit and breathtaking. He is none other than the Lord who will pronounce the solemn final judgment, 'Depart from me, you workers of lawlessness;' and not only will He pronounce it, but it will be a judgment based on people's relationship with Himself: 'I never knew you.' No wonder the original hearers were amazed, 'for he was teaching them as one who had authority, and not as their scribes' (Matt. 7:29 ESV).

The Sermon on the Mount, then, gives no sanction to the idea of a broad, ugly ditch between ethics and theology, and even less does it sanction the idea that, provided we try to live as He directed, it doesn't matter what we think about Jesus Himself. It clearly does to Him; and He is the one who will finally separate the sheep from the goats (Matt. 25:31-46).

---

2.   It is often suggested that many other teachers besides Jesus articulated the Golden Rule. There is however one important difference. His predecessors had expressed it in the negative form, 'Do not do to others what you would not wish done to yourself.' Jesus, however, expressed it positively, 'Whatever you wish that others would do to you, do also to them' (Matt. 7:12 ESV).

Accommodating ethics to culture

Finally, once we set out on the road of dismissing 'dogmas' because they are out of favour with the prevailing culture, we shall soon find ourselves doing the same with biblical ethics. This is no new thing. Since the beginning of Christendom, societies have baptised their own prejudices and preferences in the name of Christ. Some declared the burning of witches an essential part of the Christian ethic; others appealed to it in support of the divine right of kings, still others used it as a cloak to hide the evils of slavery, and Holy Willie[3] modified it to maximise the sins of others and minimise his own. South Africa practised apartheid in the name of a Christian state, and in the same name nineteenth-century Britain was still hanging homosexuals.

The point is not that ethical attitudes show a remarkable flexibility: the point is that it is fatally easy to trim our 'Christian ethic' to the prevailing wind; in the words of a canny Scotsman who suddenly saw that his principles might cost him dear, 'It's a poor conscience that'll no' bend.' When it does, morality quickly gets confused with the *mores* or customs of contemporary society.

We have already noted Adolf Harnack's impatience with Christian dogmas. The church, he argued, should content itself with preaching the universal fatherhood of God and the universal brotherhood of man. But on the very day that the First World War broke out (1st August 1914), Harnack, along with several other eminent theologians, joined ninety-three German intellectuals in issuing what Karl Barth called 'a terrible manifesto, identifying themselves before all the world with the war policy of Kaiser Wilhelm II.'[4] To Barth, who had studied under Harnack, it was like the twilight of the gods. The theology of his revered teachers had been swept away in an instant

---

3. See the poem 'Holy Willie's Prayer' in *The Canongate Burns: The Complete Poems and Songs of Robert Burns* (Edinburgh: Canongate Books, 2001), pp. 557-60.

4. Eberhard Busch, *Karl Barth: His life from letters and biographical texts*, translated by John Bowden (Eugene, Oregon: Wipf and Stock, 2005), p. 81.

by their overriding loyalty to German culture. Morality and politics, Barth realised, 'are constantly forced into concessions with reality, and therefore have no saving power in themselves.'[5]

Today, the Christian conscience, and especially the ecclesiastical conscience, continues to bend with the same ease and to make the same concessions to 'reality' that Barth found so distressing a hundred years ago. Indeed, the church has now reached such a level of indifference to the voice of the Lord and His apostles as would have shocked not only the radical modernists of the nineteenth century but even the proponents of Situation Ethics in the 1960s.[6] When the churches supported the plea that no one should be denied their *civil* rights because of their sexual orientation, that was a legitimate interpretation of their Rule of Faith; when they began to countenance the idea that homosexual practices are perfectly compatible with biblical teaching, they were fleeing in the face of a secular ethic which denies both faith and reason.

Modern Protestantism no longer sees itself as a child of the Reformation. Instead, it sees itself as a child of the Enlightenment, in which case it should remember the watchword of the Enlightenment's greatest figure, Immanuel Kant. '*Dare* to be wise,' he said (italics added).

Wisdom never goes with the flow.

---

5. *Ibid*, p. 84.

6. See Joseph Fletcher, *Situation Ethics: The New Morality* (London: SCM Press, 1966).

10

✝ THE ESCAPE TO ✝ EXPERIENCE

Believers seeking shelter from the intellectual assaults on Christianity have clearly not found it difficult, then, to find safehouses beyond the reach of such attacks. Faced with philosophical attacks on the very possibility of certainty they found refuge in the distinction between faith and knowledge. Faith was certain, even though not based on any certain knowledge. And faced with historical scepticism, they found refuge in the 'discovery' that Christianity is not a set of beliefs, but a way of life based on values which remain true and useful, regardless of the factual accuracy of the gospels, and which we could still cherish even if there never was a historical Jesus.

But there remains yet another possible safehouse. Religion, we are told, is a matter of the heart, not of the head; an experience, not a creed, and here we can feel secure because no one can ever take the experience from us. The position was summed up in the old Scottish saying, 'It's better felt than telt,' and it was reflected, too, in the religion of the Moravian Brethren, part of the eighteenth-century

Pietist reaction against a form of Protestantism which seemed to teach salvation by sound doctrine. At the heart of such Pietism lay the sentiment expressed by the prominent Moravian leader, Count Zinzendorf, 'I know it is true: my heart tells me so.'

This would certainly place the Christian faith beyond the reach of either Kant or Bultmann, but at what price? Our hearts cannot tell us, for example, whether Christ rose from the dead; without such knowledge it would be impossible to believe in Him; the only way we can get such knowledge is from the witness of the apostles; and that witness is situated in a world where every philosopher can scrutinise it and every historian cross-examine it. We have no right, then, to seek for our faith a place where criticism cannot reach it. It was, and is, a faith that produces feelings, but it was the product of facts, not feelings, these facts are in the public domain, and every aspiring scholar and every cynical teenager, has a right to express a view on them. We can't survive by claiming diplomatic immunity for our beliefs. We survive, humanly speaking, by defending the gospel (Phil.1:16) and by giving a reason for our hope (1 Pet. 3:15).

Head against heart?

But let's pause for a moment over the oft-quoted distinction between head and heart. Does Scripture sanction the idea that, while the head is the organ of only cold propositional knowledge, the heart is the organ of emotional warmth and affection, and so long as we follow our hearts everything will be OK?

One of the key biblical texts here is Genesis 6:5, 'The LORD saw that the wickedness of man was great in the earth, and that every intention of the thoughts of his *heart* was only evil continually' (ESV) (Italics added). The striking thing here is the link between the heart and the intellect. It is the heart that thinks and conceives and plans. In the first instance, the words refer to the generations before the Flood. In secular matters, they were creative innovators. They built cities; they introduced pastoral farming; they invented musical instruments; they became skilled craftsmen in bronze and iron. But in the ethical and spiritual sphere, their thoughts were only evil. They were corrupt, violent and promiscuous: all this arose from their thoughts and these thoughts, in turn, came from their hearts.

We find this pattern in Scripture repeatedly. In Isaiah 6:9, for example, it is dullness of heart that will prevent the people from understanding the prophet's message; in Jeremiah 17:9, it is the heart that is deceitful above all things and desperately wicked and, in Matthew 15:19, the Lord tells us that out of the heart come such evil thoughts as murder, adultery, false witness and slander. None of this is intended as a formal scientific psychology. The Bible's use of head-and-heart in this connection is purely metaphorical, and similar usage prevails throughout human culture. It is neither the head nor the heart that thinks (though we couldn't think without either), and in the same way it is the person, the whole person, that feels and loves and makes choices. No less certainly, our feelings and emotions are as disordered as our thoughts and perceptions. The precise relation between these various aspects of our personalities is both complex and elusive. What is clear is that sin has left no part of our humanity unaffected: not the head, and not the heart.

Letter *versus* spirit

But the distinction between head and heart is not the only one invoked by those who seek to enhance the role of the emotions at the expense of the intellect. Another distinction commonly put to the same use is that between the letter and the spirit, and, at first sight, this seems to be countenanced by the Apostle Paul when he writes, 'the letter kills, but the Spirit gives life' (2 Cor. 3:6). J. G. Machen once described this as 'the most frequently misused utterance in the whole Bible.'[1] It is certainly

---

1. J. Machen, *What Is Faith?* (London: Hodder and Stoughton, 1925), p. 187.

one instance of the way that biblical phrases can be used to support thoroughly non-biblical systems. Paul is not suggesting for a moment that the literal historical and grammatical meaning of Scripture brings death, or that it is to be discounted in favour of some deeper 'spiritual' meaning. Nor is he suggesting that there is a 'spirit of Christianity' or a 'spirit of Jesus' which is always to be preferred above the mere tenets of historic Christian theology. He is certainly not suggesting, to quote Machen again, that we must always take the Law of God with a pinch of salt and act, instead, on its 'spirit'.

The contrast Paul is drawing is not between the literal and the spiritual meanings of Scripture, but between two dispensations: the dispensation of the Law on the one hand, and the dispensation of the Spirit on the other (a fact which the ESV highlights by its use of 'Spirit' rather than 'spirit'). The Law, which said, 'Do and live,' brought death, not because of any deficiency in the Law itself but because it was 'weakened by the flesh' (Rom. 8:3). In other words, humans being humans, they couldn't rise to its standards and thus fell liable to its dread sentence, 'Cursed be everyone who does not abide by all things written in the Book of the Law, and do them' (Gal. 3:10 ESV). The underlying message is clear, 'Legalism kills,' and it kills because, while the Law, like all human moralism, can lay down principles and press home great imperatives, it has no power to ensure compliance. What, then, does Paul set over against it? Not 'the *spirit* of the Law,' but the Holy Spirit! He brings life, operating on us inwardly, transforming us at the very core of our being, bringing illumination and power, opening our eyes to see the glory of the Lord (2 Cor. 3:18), and leading us to embrace God's own righteousness: not the righteousness He demands, but the righteousness He gives (Phil. 3:9).

Far, then, from introducing the contrast between the letter and the spirit to undermine our confidence in theology and doctrine, Paul introduces it to coax us towards the most evangelical doctrine of all, justification by faith alone. Only by abandoning our endemic legalism and putting our faith in the Christ who bore our condemnation, can we experience life and freedom.

Theology and experience

But if we set aside these supposed contrasts between head and heart, letter and spirit, what then can be said of the true relation between belief and feelings, between theology and experience?

First and foremost, that Christian discipleship always involves experience: an experience, basically, of the saving power of God (Rom. 1:16). We have experienced the new birth, repentance, and being filled with the Spirit. We have experienced assurance of God's love: from temptation and fall to recovery, peace of conscience and the hope of glory. And the list could go on. We have experienced answers to prayer, moments when we were in the depths, and moments when we cried with the psalmist, 'How can God know? Is there knowledge in the Most High?' (Ps. 73:11 ESV).

Secondly, all Christian experience involves affections and feelings as well as knowledge and certainty. There is awe in the presence of God, love for the one who loved us, grief over our sins and short-comings, contentment, zeal and, above all, joy: joy in the forgive-ness of sins, joy in the hope of glory, joy in corporate worship, joy that God exists, and joy that He wants to share His own happiness with us.

Thirdly, the pursuit of blessed experiences and heart-warming feelings must never be the main preoccupation of a Christian. The temptation is very real, as Henry Scougal noted in his seventeenth-century classic, *The Life of God in the Soul of Man*. Some, he writes, 'put all religion in the affections, in rapturous hearts and ecstatic devotion, and all they aim at is to pray with passion, and think of heaven with pleasure, and to be affected with those kind and melting expressions wherewith they court their Saviour till they persuade themselves that they are mightily in love with Him, and from thence assume a great confidence of their salvation, which they esteem the chief of Christian graces.'[2]

This preoccupation with feelings and affections is still very much alive. Some still regard 'getting a blessing' as the main reason for going to church, and when they say, 'I got nothing,' what they mean is that their hearts were not warmed or their emotions stirred. Of course, worship can often be a deeply moving experience, and preaching must engage the affections (including the preacher's own) as well as the mind. But feelings can never be the main thing, though they're always welcome when they come. What the Christian disciple hungers and thirsts for, as the Lord Himself made plain, is not blessedness but righteousness (Matt. 5:6),[3] and only in that pursuit is he going to be blessed. The pursuit of happiness, as has been repeatedly stressed ever since the human race began to think, is self-defeating. We never find it except as incidental to something else. The blessed man finds it in being right with God and with his neighbour (beautifully translated in the Vulgate by the word *proximus*: my neighbour is the person next to me).

Fourth, feelings can never be the test of discipleship. For one thing, feelings in themselves are neither right nor wrong. It depends on what prompts them. The masochist takes pleasure in pain, the sadist in inflicting it, the capitalist in his money, the drunkard in his drink. The Christian aesthete gets it in the beauty of church music, the magnificence of a cathedral, the high drama of the liturgy. The

---

2. Henry Scougal, *The Life of God in the Soul of Man; or the Nature and Excellency of the Christian Religion* (1677. Reprinted with Bishop Burnet's original Preface, Aberdeen: John Rae Smith, 1892), pp. 40-41. It is only fair to add that Scougal also warns (p. 39) of the danger of reducing religion to nothing more than holding orthodox opinions and performing external duties.

3. In this connection see the sermon, 'Righteousness and Blessedness' in D. Martyn Lloyd-Jones, *Studies in the Sermon on the Mount* (2 vols., London: Inter-Varsity Fellowship, 1959), Vol. 1, pp. 73-83. It warns (p. 76) that, 'We are not meant to hunger and thirst after experiences; we are not meant to hunger and thirst after blessedness. If we want to be truly happy and blessed, we must hunger and thirst after righteousness. We must not put blessedness or happiness or experience in the first place.'

shallow-ground hearer received the message of the kingdom with joy, but his joy had no depth. The devils believe, and tremble, but although the emotion is both real and deep, it is no expression of piety. Conversely, people like Elijah or William Cowper, for all that they felt bad about themselves, were still right with God; and while the 'strange warming' that John Wesley experienced was nice while he had it, it didn't last, and he came to realise that he was as close to God after he lost it as he was while he enjoyed it.

Experience can never be either the source or the test of Christian belief. Feelings cannot tell us what we need to know, and neither can they guarantee that what we think we know is right. The Scots worthy might say, 'It's better felt than telt,' but it wasn't from his feelings that he learned that Jesus was the divine Son who had shed His blood to atone for our sins; and it wasn't his heart that informed Count Zinzendorf that Christ had risen from the dead. In the very nature of the case, these were 'mysteries' for which neither reason nor our emotional antennae could give any knowledge. Even apostles could gain such knowledge only by revelation (Gal. 1:12), and we possess it only because they passed it down to us (I Cor. 15:3).

Faith is not a source of truth, only the organ by which we receive it. Yes, we can examine faith and find out what it believes, and why. But the faith that faith believes was not generated by faith itself, but by hearing. Faith trusts a known God, and the source of that knowledge is not faith itself, but the self-revelation with which God has blessed us.

Friedrich Schleiermacher

It would be a mistake to assume, however, that the appeal to experience was confined to the pietism of Europe's peasantry. Friedrich Schleiermacher (1768–1834), often described as the father of modern Liberal Theology, likewise invoked experience as the source and norm of Christian truth. Brought up in Moravian pietism,

Schleiermacher turned his back on it as a young student and went on to become a Professor of Theology, first at the University of Halle and then at the newly established University of Berlin. One of the outstanding intellects of his age, and a master of persuasion, Schleiermacher was deeply impressed by Kant's *Critique of Pure Reason*, and particularly by its core idea that reason can provide no knowledge of God and the unseen world. Theology, he believed, had to come to terms with this. At the same time, however, himself deeply religious, he was driven by a passion to reach out to the 'cultured despisers of religion,' the philosophers, poets and scientists of nineteenth-century Germany: exactly the same concern to adapt the gospel to the tastes of the 'wise' as Paul warned against in his First Epistle to the Corinthians.

Taken together, these preoccupations led to a twofold agenda: firstly, to place religion on a scientific foundation; secondly, to show that one could be both a modern man and a religious man.

Schleiermacher found his scientific basis in what he saw as the nature of religion or piety itself. Its essence, he argued, lay neither in knowing nor in doing, but in feeling, and specifically in the feeling of absolute dependence. He recognised, of course, that everything that exists on earth is dependent on God, but it is given to man alone to feel it, and at the same time to be conscious of himself as one who exists in relation to God. Self-consciousness carries with it God-consciousness. This feeling might vary from human to human and from culture to culture, but it was a fact of human nature that we feel helpless without the Almighty, and no less so in His presence; this feeling accompanies us in all our activities, and in the whole of our existence. It was not, however, a feeling produced by some prior knowledge. The only idea of God that man possesses is what is given in the *feeling* of dependence itself.

At first sight, this seems to echo Calvin's doctrine of the 'sense' of divinity that lodges in every human heart and which provides the 'seed' from which religion grows. But there are crucial differences.

For one thing, Calvin did not present this as his own idea. He was drawing, consciously, on the teaching of Scripture, and specifically on the Apostle Paul, who, as we have seen, lays down in Romans 1:20 that the knowledge of God's 'eternal power and divinity' is engraved on every human heart. Furthermore, it was this *knowledge*, and not some feeling, that Calvin identified as the 'seed' from which all the world's religions sprang. He saw it, and the 'sense of divinity' that resulted from it, not as some natural, autonomous attribute of human nature, but as a gift of divine grace: a seed which God Himself has sown. We do indeed know of God's invisible attributes (Rom. 1:20), but we know only because God Himself has shown them to us, and what He has shown to us is not some truth about ourselves (namely, that we have a feeling of dependence) but a truth about Himself, namely, His 'eternal power and God-ness.'

But far the most important difference between Schleiermacher and Calvin is that the latter would never have regarded man's 'sense of divinity' as providing a sufficient basis for piety. In the vast majority of cases, the 'seed of religion' produces not piety, but idolatry. Piety, Calvin stressed, needs more than what we know by nature. It needs a divine word of special revelation, making known the mystery of God's utterly sovereign grace; and this is precisely what we have in Holy Scripture. Only this divine word can put the human race in touch with the news that God has sent His Son to be the propitiation for the sins of the world (1 John 2:2; 4:10).

This is why Calvin's Systematic Theology, *The Institutes of the Christian Religion*, aspires to be nothing more than a faithful and accessible summary of the teaching of the Bible, compiled in dialogue with the centuries of catholic tradition. By contrast, the corresponding work of Schleiermacher, *The Christian Faith*, owes little to the idea that Scripture is the only source of our knowledge of God and the only norm for Christian theology. Revelation, in Schleiermacher's view, was whatever providential circumstance stimulated or enhanced the feeling of absolute dependence; and in line with this, the task of theology was to reflect on this feeling, to study the self-consciousness of the pious, and to give verbal expression to their affections and feelings.

Two results follow from this. First, theology becomes anthropology: the study of human states of feeling, rather than the study of God, and secondly, religion as such has no 'tenets'. The 'Christian faith' is no longer a body of truths on which men and women venture their souls, as airline pilots put their faith in the laws of aerodynamics; rather, the key dogmas of historical Christianity can thus be safely relegated to the margins of piety. The only doctrines which need to be retained are those which were implicit in the feeling of dependence. The doctrine of the Trinity, for example, would have to be treated as a mere appendix because it seemed to have only a tenuous link with the 'feeling'. Other doctrines such as the cosmogony of Genesis, the Virgin Birth of Christ, His bodily Resurrection, Ascension, and Second Coming, would all be vulnerable; and the idea of redemption would have to be redefined. While the need for redemption was itself clearly rooted in the human self-consciousness, it no longer denoted redemption from sin and its curse. Instead, it denoted redemption from whatever obstructed the feeling of absolute dependence. The work of Christ was similarly defined in relation to this feeling. In Him, the God-consciousness exists in absolute perfection, and He redeems us by assuming believers into His own God-consciousness. The doctrine that Christ redeemed us by His blood (Rev. 1:5) is quietly eliminated, a victim to the need to win back religion's cultured despisers.

In the century after Schleiermacher, Liberal Theology underwent further development at the hands of such influential figures as Albrecht Ritschl and Adolph Harnack, but throughout these developments, it never abandoned the idea that the cultivation of 'propositional theology' borders on the impious. It would be naïve to think that this attitude left Evangelicalism unaffected. You have only to say a word in commendation of the Shorter Catechism to realise how impatient many believers are with the idea that they should be familiar with the great doctrines of the faith. The Bible is enough for them, they say, but it is this very Bible itself that urges us to progress beyond the 'milk' of the elementary doctrines of the church's missionary message to such theological 'strong meat' as the priesthood of Christ and the mystery of Melchizedek (Heb. 5:12–6:2). We are not at liberty to say, in the presence of revelation, 'Sorry, I'm not interested. I don't need to know this.'

In terms of intellectual breadth, depth and rigour, Schleiermacher's work towers above the Moravianism in which he was reared. Yet, reduced to essentials, the principle is still the same: we know only what the heart tells us, and we are sure because 'the heart tells me so'. There was, however, one vital difference. Zinzendorf's heart told him something that Schleiermacher's heart didn't tell him, namely, that the Bible was the Word of God, and that this immediately made it the source of a knowledge which the heart alone could never have yielded. Cut off from this source, doctrines which every Pietist, and every Church Father, and every Reformer, had taken for granted, disappeared not only from Liberal Protestant academies, but from Europe's pulpits and from the faith and life of its church-members. The heart alone, the feeling of dependence, could deliver only a minimalist curriculum; and foremost among the casualties was the doctrine of the Cross. Paul gloried in it. In *The Christian Faith*, it doesn't feature even in the Index.

Theologians as diverse as Charles Hodge and Karl Barth are on record as speaking warmly of Schleiermacher even while being profoundly critical of his theology. During his time in Berlin in 1827, Hodge heard Schleiermacher preach and, based on his own experience and on the testimony of his Evangelical friends in Germany, he declared many years later that he was 'a devout worshipper of Christ'. The explanation may be that some of Schleiermacher's Moravian background stayed with him throughout his life, and that this came through in his preaching, but it is tempting here to insert Robert McCheyne's comment on hearing of the death of Edward Irving: 'He is now with his God and Saviour, whom he wronged so much, yet, I am persuaded, loved so sincerely.'[4] Schleiermacher certainly positioned the Christian faith where it seemed safe from the criticisms of sceptical philosophers and equally sceptical historians, but only at the cost of turning it into 'another gospel' (Gal. 1:6). Stripped of its 'tenets' it became, at the hands of his successors, a bland humanitarianism more concerned to keep in step with the prevailing culture than to keep in step with the New Testament. The ironical result was that an enterprise designed to win over religion's 'cultured despisers' succeeded only in emptying the Protestant churches.

Beliefs produce experience

The natural relation of doctrine to feeling is not that feeling produces doctrines but that doctrines produce feelings (and good Christian practice).[5] This is certainly what we find in Scripture: cognition leads to emotion. To quote just a few examples: the perception of the holiness of God leads to self-abasement (Isa. 6:5, Ps. 32:3-4); the doctrine of justification by faith gives us peace (Rom. 5:1); God's gift of His Son to be an atoning sacrifice for our sins leads us to love Him (1 John 4); the word about the Parousia and the resurrection comforts us in our grief (1 Thess. 4:18); the knowledge that we have a great High Priest leads to boldness before the Throne (Heb. 4:14-16); the knowledge of God's fatherly care allays anxiety (Matt. 6:32); the knowledge that labour in the Lord is not in vain produces zeal (1 Cor. 15:58); the knowledge that we are God's children induces us

---

4. Irving had been deposed from the ministry of the Church of Scotland in 1833 for teaching that the human nature of Christ had the same sinful propensities as were to be found in other human beings, the difference being that in him they were held in check by the power of the Holy Spirit. He died in 1834.

5. It may be worth noting that Christopher Columbus would never have set off on his historic voyage had it not been for his faith in the newly discovered doctrine that the earth is round, not flat.

to purify ourselves as He is pure (1 John 3:3); the knowledge of the greatness of God leads to jubilation (Ps. 95:1-7).

None of this means, however, that feeling and affection are less important than intellect and cognition. There is no room in biblical psychology for any such grading. Knowledge without emotion would be sterile. 'The Author of the human nature,' wrote Jonathan Edwards, 'has not only given affections to men, but has made them very much the spring of men's actions .... Such is man's nature, that he is very inactive, any otherwise than he is influenced by some affection, either love or hatred, desire, hope, fear, or some other.'[6] This is why, as Edwards emphasises, the preacher must present his message in a way that not only enlightens the mind but stirs the affections.

We also need to bear in mind that the relationship between knowledge and experience is not a one-way one. Emotion may not produce truth, but it can stimulate the search for it. All Evangelicals are familiar with the story, already referred to, of John Wesley's experience at a meeting in Aldersgate, London, on 24th May, 1738. 'I felt,' he recorded, 'my heart strangely warmed.'[7] Many since have longed for just such an experience, but we need to remember that the 'warming' didn't suddenly come from nowhere. It came because, at that point in the meeting, someone was reading from Luther's Preface to the Epistle to the Romans. Wesley had gone to the meeting 'very unwillingly', and was clearly in a state of spiritual distress, lamenting his 'dulness, coldness, and unusually frequent lapses into sin.' He was still relying on his own 'religion by method' and still ignorant of the 'righteousness of Christ' as described in Philippians 3:8-9. But precisely because of his distress, he was looking for relief, and he found it in Luther's Preface where the Reformer called for 'a living, daring confidence in God's grace.' Yes, we are still sinners, Luther

---

6. Edwards, *Affections*, p. 29.
7. *The Journal of John Wesley*, Vol. 1, pp. 475-6.

remarked, because the flesh is not slain, 'but because we believe in Christ and have a beginning of the Spirit, God is so favourable and gracious to us that he will not count the sin against us or judge us because of it. Rather he deals with us according to our faith in Christ, until sin is slain.'[8] It was this doctrine, the doctrine of justification by faith in Christ, that warmed Wesley's heart and, when the feeling passed (as it did), the doctrine was still true.

We find exactly the same situation in the story of the two disciples on the Road to Emmaus on Easter morning (Luke 24:13-35). When they first meet the risen Lord they are 'sad' (v. 17): disillusioned and completely demoralised. All their hopes have been buried with Jesus. After their conversation with Him, their hearts are burning within them and, all fired-up, they immediately retrace their steps and repeat the seven-mile journey back to Jerusalem to share the news with the Eleven (who, by the time they reach them, already know). What accounts for this dramatic change in attitude? Two things: firstly, the fact that the Lord had risen and, secondly, the way that He had opened up the Scriptures and illuminated the Messianic message proclaimed by Moses and all the prophets. Cognition made their hearts burn within them, and we find exactly the same sequence in Peter's recollection of his own experience. His hope, too, had died at the cross, but God had revived it (and him) by raising Christ from the dead (1 Pet. 1:3). Nothing could ever change that; and it could not, and must not, be kept private. It must be 'telt as well as felt.'

Yet not by human voice only. We, as Cowper reminds us, have but 'poor, lisping, stammering tongues,' totally powerless to pene-trate human resistance to God's news about His Son. If Christ had had no one to plead His cause except preachers and missionaries, it would have perished long since. But from the beginning, it had another Advocate, the Holy Spirit, commissioned for the very purpose of empowering the messengers (Acts 1:8), convincing

---

8. *Luther's Works*, Vol. 35, p. 370.

the world (John 16:8) and glorifying Christ (John 16:14). This does not absolve us of responsibility. We must preach the Good News (1 Pet. 1:13), and that burden can certainly create a 'feeling of absolute dependence.' But if we put our dependence in the right place, then the gospel will reach our audiences 'not only in word, but also in power and in the Holy Spirit and with full conviction' (1 Thess. 1:5 ESV).

Conclusion

Tempting though it is, then, we have no right to seek for our faith some inaccessible inner place where hostility and criticism cannot reach it. It was, and is, a faith that produces feelings, but it was itself produced by news and by facts, not by feelings; these facts are in the public domain and every passer-by has a right to express a view on them. We cannot survive by claiming that faith is a purely personal matter warranted only by our own private and incommunicable experience. In its very nature, it is a faith which, together with its warrant, is to be preached to every nation and to every creature (Matt. 28:19): a faith which we are to defend (Phil.1:16) and for which we are prepared to give reasons (1 Pet. 3:15)

This doesn't mean that every believer must be able to challenge the arguments of a David Hume or a Richard Dawkins, but it does mean that each one of us should be able, with the help of the Spirit, to give those we mix with an explanation for our personal convictions. And it means, too, that part of the responsibility of our pastors and teachers is to equip us to do precisely that. We must be ready to fight off any giants we may meet on the way.

11

✢ ALL TOGETHER IN ✢
ONE PLACE

When I say, 'I believe,' I am clearly making a personal statement. But should it also be a private one, valid between myself and my Maker, but not something that anyone else need know about, or to which I should give any public or visible expression?

This is certainly the way that modern Western society would like things to be. It is bad form to introduce religion into a conversation, and even worse (and dangerous) to introduce it into your CV; and, following on from this, there is no reason why being a believer should entail being a member of any church. Christianity is one thing, institutional religion quite another. For the Christian pilgrim, it is best to travel alone.

This is why, of all the articles of the Apostles' Creed, the one most ignored by modern Evangelicals is the one in which we affirm, 'I believe in the holy, catholic church.' Even before the current Coronavirus pandemic, many were attempting to live their Christian lives without any church-connection: some because they'd fallen in with the prevailing culture of individualism and personal self-sufficiency; some because of a distrust of all institutions; some because of what they saw as doctrinal and moral impurities in the church. Some because of its failure to adopt their own particular shibboleths; others because they'd been hurt by the church; yet others because of tensions between them and other members of their congregations; still others because they 'get nothing' out of going to church.

These currents were already running strongly before the world was hit by Covid-19, but the pandemic has given them new force. The prohibition on religious gatherings (as on others) provided a good excuse for those who were growing weary of church; others quickly grew accustomed to the live-streaming of their local services and fell in love with the idea that you could now go to church without 'going to church'; yet others discovered that celebrity on-line evangelists were (at least on first acquaintance) far better preachers than their own local ministers (and their praise-bands better still).

A divine institution

But the church is not a voluntary body which I may choose to join or not to join at my own discretion. It is a divine institution because, from the very beginning, it was God's will that those bearing His name should live, not as spiritual soloists, but as His own special people, living as a distinct community under one Law, sharing the same blessings, following the same order of worship, and charged with the same commission. Under the Old Testament, He formed them into 'the congregation of the Lord;' under the New, they form what Christ called 'my church'. Here, He is already using the word *ecclesia*, which was to become the standard New Testament term for the church.

In secular Greek, it meant an assembly, as we can see in Luke's account of the riot in Ephesus when, he tells us, the assembly (*ecclesia*) was in confusion. It was the usual term for formal public assemblies in such city-states as Athens when the citizens came together to make political decisions. In the Septuagint, *ecclesia* translates the Hebrew word, *qahal,* as in the phrase 'the assembly of the Lord,' which older English versions such as the Geneva Bible translated as 'the *congregation* of the Lord'. On this analogy, when Christ spoke of 'my church' His words might well have been translated, 'my congregation.'[1] Another Hebrew term, *'edah,* referred more broadly to the whole community of Israel, whether assembled or not. This was translated by the Greek word *synagogē,* which not only embodied the idea of people meeting together, but also denoted those entitled to come to the meeting. In this sense, the synagogue continued to exist even after it dispersed, and the same is true of Christ's congregation. The church doesn't exist only on Sundays. It is still the body of Christ during the week.

A holy convocation

All these terms express the same core idea: God has His own special people, and they form an assembly or congregation which regularly meets together. But behind both the Hebrew and Greek words for the church, there also lies the idea of a divine call.[2] The church is a holy convocation which has been called into being by God, it meets in response to His summons, and every believer is bound to obey.

This was clearly the position of Old Testament Israel. God had made them His people, and in accordance with His commandment, they would celebrate their feasts, observe their fasts, and go up to the Temple, not as separate individuals, but together; and it is this same pattern that we see in the life of the New Testament church. No one can emerge from even a cursory reading of the Book of

---

1.   Cf. the practice of the Brethren, who spoke not of the congregation but of 'the meeting'.

2.   The noun *ecclesia* is derived from the verb *ekkaleo,* meaning 'I call out'; the Hebrew *qahal* also appears as a verb which, in its active or causal form, means to call or summon (an assembly).

Acts still believing that Christian discipleship consists of nothing more than 'a personal relationship with Jesus.' It also involves a personal relationship with His people, and in line with this, the practice of public commitment to a special, Spirit-filled community was established on Day One when the three thousand people who gladly received Peter's word on the Day of Pentecost were not only baptised immediately, but were also, as Luke puts it, 'added' to the existing body of believers (Acts 2:41).

A solitary, individual, self-sufficient and invisible discipleship was clearly not to be the Christian pattern. Instead, driven by an inner impulse, and in submission to apostolic authority, the believers immediately bonded together and formed a distinct visible community of men and women who met together publicly and frequently for four great objects: to receive instruction in apostolic doctrine, to share gifts and resources, to break bread, and to pray (Acts 2:42).

At the same time, however, Luke's language makes plain that they were not establishing something new. They were 'added' to a community that already existed, and that had been called into being by Christ Himself. John the Baptist was a loner, but from the very beginning, Jesus surrounded Himself with disciples, not only to train them to be His apostles, but 'to be with him' (Mark 3:14): so very, very human, and echoing, in its own different context, the words of Genesis 2:18, 'It is not good for man to be alone.' First, He called Peter and Andrew, James and John; then Philip and Nathanael; and soon afterwards, Matthew the tax collector and the rest of the Twelve. These formed the nucleus of His congregation, and by the end of His ministry, His followers ('those running after Jesus,' as someone put it) also included the women who followed Him from Galilee to Jerusalem and became the first witnesses to His resurrection. By the time of His Ascension, there were at least five hundred 'brothers' (1 Cor. 15:6). Then, as they waited at Jerusalem for the promised gift of the Holy Spirit (Acts 1:4-5), the company kept gathering for prayer, and this is probably how they were occupied on the Day of Pentecost when, suddenly, there came 'a sound like a mighty rushing wind,' they were all filled with the Spirit, and they began to proclaim in 'other' tongues the mighty works of God (Acts 2:11 ESV).

It was to this company of the original followers of Jesus that the three thousand converts were 'added;' and having been added, they devoted themselves, as we have seen, to the apostles' teaching, to fellowship, to the breaking of bread and to the prayers (Acts 2:42): 'a beautiful little cameo of the Spirit-filled church,' as John Stott called it.[3] But little though it is, the picture is also a perfect one, and every element within it is essential. It is not only a thing of beauty; it is a God-given norm. As the gospel spread from Jerusalem to Galilee and Samaria, and then to Antioch, Galatia, Ephesus, Corinth, Rome, Alexandria, Tunisia, Constantinople, Spain, France and Britain, wherever there were disciples, there were churches; and when they met together, their meetings already had order and purpose. They assembled for the precise objects specified in the 'little cameo,' and these are still the reasons why God requires us to meet together today.

They came together for teaching

First, we come together to be taught, and when Luke says that the early believers 'devoted themselves' to it, he means that they were enthusiastic about it. They longed to gather every possible scrap of information about their Lord and His teaching; and they longed, too, to hear how He expected them to live.[4] But to learn, they had to come together, gathered around authorised and authoritative teachers. The Lord Himself was no longer physically present to teach

---

3. John R. W. Stott, *The Message of Acts* (Leicester: Inter-Varsity Press, 1991), p.81. Cf. Calvin, 'Do we seek the true Church of Christ? The picture of it is here painted to the life' (*The Acts of the Apostles 1-13*, tr. John W. Fraser and W. J. G. McDonald; Grand Rapids: Eerdmans, 1995), p. 85.

4. The Great Commission highlights not only the importance of making disciples, but also the importance of teaching Jesus' commandments (Matt. 28:20).

them, but He had commissioned the apostles to be His messengers, and their word was His word.

Today, the apostles themselves are no longer with us but, being dead, they still speak through their gospels and their epistles. Nor is that all. They also instituted an order of pastor/teachers (Eph. 4:11-12) to ensure that after their decease believers would still be taught. Such pastor-teachers are no less a divine institution than the church herself,[5] and so long as they content themselves with expounding the apostolic message, their word is the apostles' word, just as the apostles' word was the Lord's word. This is the true Apostolic Succession, distinguished, not by the vestments people wear or the ceremonies by which they've been appointed to office, but by unremitting toil as self-effacing teachers of the apostolic gospel.

But at the same time, Pentecost set clear precedents: the primary setting for receiving such instruction was to be the church, the assembly of believers; or, putting it the other way round, the reason for gathering together was, first and foremost, to be taught.[6] Like the teaching of the Lord Himself, the teaching was to be largely oral. Later, men like Peter would write as well as preach, giving us the New Testament as we have it today, and the stimulus produced by their writings would give rise to the great body of theological literature which is still such a precious part of our Christian heritage. Later still, Christian teachers at the time of the Reformation would make brilliant use of the printing press; and now, in the twenty-first century, God has given access to even greater audiences through the electronic media. But face-to-face oral preaching, in the setting of the church, and in the light of the Lord's promise to be present in a special way wherever two or three meet together in His name (Matt. 18:20) still remains God's ordained way of leading believers into an ever-

---

5. 'A foundational part of our discipleship is to be served the means of grace by the ministers God has gifted to his church' (Aimee Byrd, *Recovering from Biblical Manhood and Womanhood*; Grand Rapids: Zondervan, 2020), p. 142.

6. Cf. Calvin's comment that teaching is 'the soul of the church' (*Ibid,* p. 85).

deepening understanding of their faith. The printed word, and the on-line word, may be extensions of it, but they can never replace it.

It was by such teaching, and in such a setting, that believers were to grow towards spiritual maturity (Eph.4:13). By it they were to be sanctified (John 17:17), by it they would comfort one another (1 Thess. 4:18), by it they would learn how to give a reason for their hope (1 Pet. 3:15), by it they would learn how God required them to live, and by it they would be led to long for the day when they would see Christ not, as now, through a glass darkly, but face to face.

Fellowship

Yet, 'School of Christ' though it is, the church can never be just a school, far less a mere theological club. Believers need more and, as the 'little cameo' makes plain, preaching must never stand alone or be divorced from the other practices which graced the gatherings of the church in the days following Pentecost.

The first of these was fellowship. Today, the idea has shrunk to the point where it means no more than an informal Christian get-together. In Acts 2:42, however, the meaning is much deeper, and at its heart lies the word *koine*, the Greek adjective for 'common.' Christians shared a common life, based on a common faith. They had one Lord; they were all united to Christ; they were all filled with His Spirit; and when they gathered together, they did so as brothers and sisters, sons and daughters of the one Father in heaven. They had all experienced repentance and baptism, and in the years to come they would all share persecution together, experience the care of the Chief Shepherd together, derive comfort and encouragement from each other, serve as examples to each other, and be enriched by the *charismata* which God had lavished on individual members for the benefit of the whole body (1 Cor. 12:1-11).

But it wasn't only a fellowship of receiving. It was also a fellowship of giving. All their resources were made available for the benefit of the whole community. Such notes as, 'I can do what I want with my own,' were not to be heard. They made their homes available for the Breaking of Bread and for the apostles' ministry of teaching (Acts 2:46); they sold their properties and valuables to ensure that none of their number was in need.[7] As the gospel moved beyond both Jerusalem and Judaism, traditional barriers of race, class, and gender would be broken down. Every man was a brother, and every woman a sister; each would have the opportunity to serve, each would be needed, and each would be appreciated.

And what was true of relations within particular local churches was to be equally true of relations between churches. They would constitute one church (Eph. 4:4), transcending national, ethnic and geographical barriers. They would pray for each other, exchange greetings and letters of recommendation (Rom. 16:16, 2 Cor. 3:1), and worship in accordance with the same apostolic guidelines (1 Cor. 11:23-32, 14:26-40). Above all, they would provide mutual help and support in times of distress, as the Gentile churches of Antioch, Macedonia and Achaia did when they contributed with self-denying generosity to the collection for the poor believers in far-away Jerusalem (Acts 11:29, 2 Cor. 8:1-15).

This common life would be a unity of heart and mind: a unity of shared belief, shared endeavour and shared suffering. In the very highest sense, believers would never walk alone, nor ever follow Christ on their own.

It was a high ideal, and we know that it did not maintain for long the perfection which marked its beginning. The church was the New Israel, but it was not yet the New Jerusalem, protected by a great high wall (Rev. 21:12). The Serpent could still get in, and quickly did. Yet the cameo of Acts 2:42 remains the divine norm for the church of all ages, reminding us that all Christians share a common life, and providing a paradigm for the way the Lord expects

---

7.   This was an adaptation of the policy of the common purse which was a clear feature of the life of Jesus while He was with His disciples in the days of His flesh.

individual believers, local churches (and, in our current fragmented state, separate denominations) to relate to each other. Let's never forget John Wesley's warning against amusing the world 'with the spots of God's children.'[8] The Moravians, he said, had critics enough without British Christians adding their voices.

The breaking of bread

Another key feature of the 'little cameo' was 'the breaking of bread.' There is general agreement that the phrase refers to the Lord's Supper, usually celebrated in various homes, and possibly in the setting of an ordinary meal (Acts 2:46). They may well have wished that they could all enjoy it together, but it would have been impossible to find a private venue large enough to accommodate 3,000 communicants, and out of the question to administer the Sacrament in their usual public meeting-place, Solomon's Portico on the eastern side of the Outer Court of the Temple.[9] The location wasn't important then, and it isn't important now. It is worth reminding ourselves, however, that those who gathered for the Breaking of Bread had already been baptised. Both sacraments had been solemnly instituted by Christ, and neither then nor now are His followers at liberty to dispense with either of them. We are to believe in them, and receive them, as solemnly instituted divine ordinances. There can be no sacrament-less Christian discipleship.

To some extent, of course, the Breaking of Bread (like Baptism) was a boundary-marker, and sharing in it was a courageous statement of allegiance not only to the apostles, but to the Christ they preached. Men had crucified Him, and in the world's eyes He was a disgraced Messianic Pretender, but God had reversed the human verdict, raised Him from the dead, and exalted Him to His own right hand. The

---

8. *The Journal of the Rev. John Wesley, A. M.* (Vol. 1, London: Robert Culley, 1909), p. 429.

9. See F. F. Bruce, *The Acts of the Apostles: the Greek Text with Introduction and Commentary* (London: Tyndale Press, Second Edition, 1952), pp. 107, 137.

Sacrament was more, however, than an act of witness. It was also an expression of the common life they shared with Christ and with each other. Gathered as they were in His name (Matt. 18:20), they expected the risen and exalted Jesus to be at the Breaking of Bread with them; but the sacrament also highlighted the fact that what lay at the basis of their common life was that they all shared in the one bread of life and in the one cup of the covenant blood. Yet even this was not all. In the sacrament there was a remembrance of His death and an anticipation of His coming again, but there was also His own precious invitation, 'Take, eat. This is my body, which is for you'; and with the mouth of faith they would take *Him*, together, and find their wonder and gratitude rekindled, and their spiritual energy renewed.

It was a simple ceremony, yet it is clear from 1 Corinthians 11:17-34 that it is not a matter of indifference how the Sacrament is administered. Here, too, we are subject to the test of apostolicity, and particularly to the instructions St Paul gives in 1 Corinthians 11:23-32. These can be reduced to one clear principle: our Order for Communion must follow the order of the Last Supper, omitting nothing that Christ instituted, and adding no embellishment that He hasn't sanctioned. The elements must be those which He himself blessed, bread and wine; the form must be that of a supper, around a table (Lk. 22:14), not of a sacrificial offering around an altar. There must be a prayer of thanksgiving and, just as preaching cannot stand alone without the sacrament, so the sacrament cannot stand alone without preaching which links the Sacrament back to the Lord's death and forward to His return (1 Cor. 11:26).

This what Augustine meant when he declared that, without the Word, the water of Baptism is neither more nor less than water, and the bread of the Supper is neither more nor less than bread. Only when the Word is added to the element, do you have the Sacrament.[10]

---

10. Augustine, *Homilies on the Gospel of Saint John*, LXXX:3 (*The Nicene and Post-Nicene Fathers*, ed. Philip Schaff, 1888. Reprinted Edinburgh, T&T Clark, 1991), p. 344.

We must receive Baptism and the Lord's Supper not as mysteries, but with true understanding.[11] 'The sacraments,' writes Calvin, 'take their virtue from the Word, when it is preached intelligibly. Without this, they are unworthy to be called sacraments.'[12] We have to understand that the Supper is not an ordinary meal, but a sacred occasion, graced by the presence of the Lord Himself; we have to understand that there is no magical power in the elements; we have to understand that here all barriers of race, class and learning cease to exist; we have to understand that we come as sinners who have faced the truth about ourselves and are in continuous need of forgiveness.

Above all, our approach to the Table must be in line with the purposes for which Christ instituted the Sacrament. We come to give thanks for the broken body and the shed blood (hence the term 'Eucharist'); we come to keep alive the remembrance of the Lord's life and work; we come to share in the fellowship of giving and receiving, accepting the gift of the bread and wine from our neighbour, and passing it to the one next to us; finally, we come, as we would to any meal, because we are hungry: hungry for spiritual food, the bread of life.

To list these things should be enough to remind us that Communion cannot be celebrated perfunctorily. It must be given time; and while it should indeed be a moment of sacred solemnity, it should also be a moment of exuberant joy (Acts 2:46) in which the Lord commands all believers to participate: '*This do*, in remembrance of me' (Luke 22:19).

The prayers

The final element in the 'little cameo' was 'the prayers,' meaning in this case common or shared prayer. It goes without saying that they

---

11.   While such language as 'the *mystery* of the Lord's Supper' became current in later theology, there is no precedent for it in the New Testament.

12.   *Calvin: Theological Treatises*, tr. John K. S. Reid (London: SCM Press, 1954), p. 161. Here, 'virtue' means power.

also engaged in private prayer, but it's also notable that, in the very early days, Christians continued to observe the set times of prayer at the Temple. Acts 3:1 (ESV), for example, records that 'Peter and John were going up to the temple at the hour of prayer, the ninth hour': a clear sign that the apostles did not immediately break with the Synagogue but continued to live as observant Jews. To have done otherwise at this stage in their mission to the world would merely have aroused prejudices. We can be sure, however, that, though they observed Jewish hours, the prayers themselves were Christian in form and content.

But the reference in Acts 2:42 is neither to private prayer nor to the set prayers of Jewish worship. It is a reference to the fact that the early Christians were devoted to praying together; and 'together' seems to have meant gatherings in their various homes (Acts 12:12). This doesn't necessarily mean what we today would call prayer-meetings, arranged for the sole purpose of praying. It is clear that the homes were also used for both teaching and the breaking of bread (Acts 2:46), and probably all three took place at the same time, each informing the other. We can also assume that it was to these gatherings that people brought the proceeds of what they had sold (Acts 2:34).

It was to one such meeting that Peter and John repaired following their release from detention after the miraculous healing of the Lame Beggar (Acts 3:1-10). On that occasion, the Jewish authorities, unable to deny the miracle (and very much aware that news of this 'notable sign' had all Jerusalem agog), released the two apostles with the warning that they must never preach the name of Jesus again; whereupon Peter and John immediately made their way to the home where they knew their friends were gathered. Their report prompted an immediate chorus of prayer (Acts 4:23-4), and we can be sure that the hours of the night had been devoted to the same activity.

But the respite was to be brief. Stephen's powerful preaching quickly led to his martyrdom, and to a campaign of persecution so intense that the believers were forced to flee from Jerusalem. Herod Agrippa, the king, then joined in, ordering the execution of James, the brother of John; and when he saw that this went down well with the Jews, he ordered the arrest of Peter, intending, no doubt, to have him put to death in the morning. In the meantime, however, 'earnest prayer for him was made to God by the church' (Acts 12:5 ESV). The praying must have continued well into the night, because Peter was sound asleep when an angel came to rescue him; and when he then made his way to the house of Mary, the mother of John Mark, he found the church still there, praying.[13]

We read of no further angelic missions to rescue persecuted believers, and Peter clearly did not presume on such miracles being repeated. Instead, he fled to Caesarea, as the Lord had sanctioned.[14] But then, in one of the great ironies of history, it became the turn of Paul, the converted persecutor, to ask believers to pray for himself as 'a prisoner for the Lord' (Eph. 4:1) and 'an ambassador in chains' (Eph. 6.20).

This remains a standing order for the church: 'Remember those who are in prison, as though in prison with them' (Heb. 13:3 ESV). In post-Reformation Scotland, public worship was governed by Knox's *Book of Common Order,* and a key feature of that Order was that prayer was to be made every Lord's Day for the 'Whole Estate of Christ's Church', and particularly for 'our brethren which are persecuted, cast in prison, and daily condemned to death for the testimony of thy truth.' Ministers were not bound to use the exact words of the *Book,* but they were directed to use 'this prayer following, or such like', and it is worth quoting in full:

Though they be utterly destitute of all man's aid, yet let thy sweet comfort never depart from them, but so inflame their hearts with thy

---

13.   It is ironical, as John Stott points out, 'that the group who were praying fervently and persistently for Peter's deliverance should regard as mad the person who informed them that their prayers had been answered! Rhoda's simple joy shines brightly against the dark background of the church's incredulity' (*The Message of Acts,* p. 211).

14.   'When they persecute you in one town, flee to the next' (Matt. 10:23 ESV).

Holy Spirit, that they may boldly and cheerfully abide such trial as thy godly wisdom shall appoint. So that at length, as well by their death as by their life, the kingdom of thy dear Son Jesus Christ may increase and shine through all the world.

To Knox, who had had to flee from England to escape Mary Tudor's deadly hatred of Protestantism, persecution was a recent memory, and in such countries as France, Spain and Italy, it still raged with grim ferocity as despotism threw all the resources of tyranny into the project of extinguishing the Reformation. Today, Christians in the Western world enjoy relative peace, but this should not blind us to the fact that, even in the twenty-first century, millions of our spiritual brothers and sister live under the lash. Their suffering should cast a shadow of grief, and a light of admiration, over all our Sunday Services.

12

✝ I BELIEVE IN THE HOLY ✝ CATHOLIC CHURCH

In the centuries after the apostles, the church retained its place at the heart of Christian life, and when men turned their minds to forming what we know today as the ecumenical creeds, they placed at the heart of them the clear affirmation, 'I believe in the holy catholic church.' Such was the language of the Nicene Creed and such, too, was the language of the Apostles Creed,[1] on which Martin Luther commented, 'Christian truth could not possibly be put into a shorter and clearer statement'.[2] It is a summary of those fundamental

---

1. So called, not because it was composed by the apostles, but because it set forth the apostolic gospel. Although in use from the late fourth century for the instruction of candidates for baptism, the text as we know it today was finalised only in the eighth. It came to be widely used at baptismal services as a public statement of the faith being professed, and this practice continued after the Reformation. *Knox's Liturgy*, for example, lays down that 'the Father shall rehearse the Articles of his Faith; which done, the Minister expoundeth the same.' Although not the work of an Ecumenical Council, the Apostles' Creed has been recognised throughout Christendom as a confessional formula of equal authority with the creeds of Nicea and Chalcedon.

2. Quoted in the article 'Creeds' in *New Dictionary of Theology*, ed. Sinclair B. Ferguson and David F. Wright (Leicester: Inter-Varsity Press, 1988).

doctrines which have been believed, and are to be believed, by all Christians; and among these fundamentals stands this, 'I believe in the holy catholic church.'

It is safe to say that, of all the Articles of the Creed, this is the one most neglected by modern Evangelicals, yet here it sits in distinguished company, side by side with a declaration of faith 'in God, the Father Almighty' and in 'Jesus Christ, his Son, our Lord'; and no less remarkable is that it is placed between the declaration of faith in the Holy Spirit on the one side, and faith in the forgiveness of sins and the resurrection of the body on the other. There could be no clearer indication of historic Christianity's belief in the importance of the church to Christian discipleship.

There is but one church

But what does this Article say? First of all, that we believe, not in many churches, but in one. This one church has, of course, many local manifestations, each reflecting the language, culture, history and demography of its own location; and over and above these unavoidable variations, there are also, tragically, others created by the countless schisms and heresies which have left her 'sore distressed', and by the plethora of parties which flourish even under the umbrella of nominal denominational unity.

But none of this can take away from the fact that the one God has but one people; that the one Christ has but one body, and speaks, not of building my *churches*, but of building my *church* (Matt. 16:18); that St Peter can describe God's widely dispersed elect as *one* chosen race, *one* holy nation, and *one* people for God's own special possession (1 Pet. 1:9); or that St Paul can speak of one 'household of God' (Eph. 2:19 esv).

This oneness finds expression in such features as unity of doctrine, baptism in the name of the one Lord, and the celebration of the one Sacrament of Remembrance (1 Cor. 11:25). But what ultimately binds us together is neither shared sacraments nor unity of doctrine, but our common experience of the new birth and our adoption as members of God's family. Schism may, indeed, rend the church asunder, but nothing can fracture the bond, the organic bond, that links every believer to every other believer. We can offend against the unity of the family, but we can never undo it.

This should not blind us, however, to the disorder that marks us today, where believers living side by side refuse to worship together, and instead form separate organisations, meeting in separate buildings, from which the singing of the same psalms can be clearly heard every Sunday morning by the cynical passer-by.

But then, precisely because there is but one church, it follows that, outside of it, there is no salvation. This is what Calvin meant when, following the Church Father, Cyprian,[3] he wrote that whoever has God for his Father has the church for his Mother;[4] it is what the Westminster Confession (25:2) meant when it declared that outside the church 'there is no ordinary possibility of salvation'.

By inserting the word 'ordinary', the Confession did indeed allow for exceptions: for example, those dying in infancy,[5] and that very small number of human beings who, because of cognitive limitations, cannot be reached by either the word or the sacraments. Such exceptions apart, however, the principle remains that away from the church 'one cannot hope for any forgiveness of sins or any salvation,'[6] and the fundamental reason for this is that only from the church can we learn what we need to know in order to be saved. Through her, we received the Bible; through her, we heard the Word

---

3. Cyprian, *On the Unity of the Catholic Church*, vi, 'He can no longer have God for his Father, who has not the Church for his Mother.' (*The Ante-Nicene Fathers*, Vol. 5; Grand Rapids: Eerdmans, 1995), p. 423.

4. *Institutes*, IV:I, 1.

5. See, for example, the categorical statement of A. A. Hodge, 'All the members of the human race dying in infancy are believed to be saved through the merits of Christ.' *The Confession of Faith: A Handbook of Christian Doctrine Expounding the Westminster Confession* (1869. Reprinted London: Banner of Truth, 1958), p. 314.

6. Calvin, *Institutes*, IV:I, 4.

preached; through her, God sent us missionaries and evangelists; through her, we were introduced to the gospel as children.

Yet the principle, 'outside the church there is no salvation,' doesn't mean that all conversions depend on contact with the *institutional* church. The one categorical principle is that we can never be saved unless we 'truly come to Christ' (*Westminster Confession*, 10:4); linked to this is a second, namely, that we shall never come unless the Father draws us (John 6:44); linked to this again there is a third, that God has absolute discretion as to the means by which He draws us. It may be that, like Timothy, the gospel was handed down to us by our mothers and grandmothers (2 Tim. 1:5); or that in the workplace we heard colleagues casually 'speaking the word' (Acts 11:19 ESV);[7] or that 'accidentally' we found a Bible, or even a few pages of it; or that a solitary Christian pedlar spoke of Jesus as he travelled through the unevangelised fields of north-east India; or that Roman soldiers serving in the remote province of ancient Britain found opportunities to speak of Jesus to the native population. None of these represents organised missionary activity on the part of the institutional church, but in every instance, and in one way or another, God used His people to bring us that knowledge of Christ without which we could never have come to faith.

But not only is the church our Mother in the sense that it was through her that we were born into the family of God: it is also through the church that believers are nourished in the faith from the earliest days of spiritual infancy to the final moment when growth gives way to glory. No matter how dramatic and memorable our conversion, and no matter how personally gifted we may be, discipleship will wither on the vine unless we follow God's order, cherish the gifts and fellowship of our co-believers and join together with them for teaching, the breaking of bread, and prayers. Each of

---

7. This should not be regarded as 'exceptional'. As we have seen, it was through such 'amateur missionaries' that God planted the church at Antioch which quickly became the metropolis of early Gentile Christianity.

us individually is indebted to the whole church: to the apostles and prophets who still speak to us through the holy Scriptures; to the preachers through whom we were led to faith; to pastor-teachers whom the risen Lord has given us precisely to build us up towards spiritual maturity; to all the brothers and sisters who admonished us when we were out of order, encouraged us when were depressed, and helped us when we were weak (I Thess. 5:14).

The church is holy

Secondly, we believe that this one church is holy, and that this is an attribute not simply of the individuals who compose it, but of the community itself. Just as Israel of old was God's own people, holy to Himself, so the church is a holy nation (I Pet. 2:9); or, as Paul puts it, we are the holy temple of God (I Cor. 3:17). Precisely because God is a God like no other, so the church is a community like no other community on earth. It is 'wholly other,' called out from the world, and differing from it in the beliefs it holds, the priorities it targets, the ethics it lives by, and the values it cherishes; different, too, in the qualities it requires in its leaders and in the methods it relies on to propagate and defend its faith. Above all, it is different in the reasons for its existence: not to build its own empires, but to extol the virtues of Christ (I Pet. 2:9), to extend His kingdom (Matt. 28:19), to deliver His message of reconciliation (2 Cor 5:18), to give public and visible embodiment to the unique form of righteousness that He preached (Matt. 5:16), to intercede for the communities we live in (I Tim. 2:2, Jer. 29:7), and to urge humanity to view history from its end point, the universal judgment of God (Heb. 9:27).

It is also holy in that it consists of saints: individuals whom God has set aside to be His own special people and who are distinguished from the world, not by being more virtuous or more wise or more rational in the conventional human sense, but by being filled with God's Spirit, keeping in step with Him throughout their lives, and showing their love for Christ by keeping His commandments (John 14:15).

Yet, mixed in with the saints, and often indistinguishable from them, are others of a different character, as the history of the early churches clearly shows. All had hypocrites, all had heretics, all had members whose real love was the world, all had people who, after showing great early promise, soon showed that they had no spiritual staying power, and all had would-be leaders who saw themselves as super-spiritual and looked down on their fellow believers.

But this should not betray us into the cynical conclusion that all Christians are hypocrites, nor should it foster the illusion that if we put proper safeguards in place we can ensure that only true believers are admitted to the church's membership. There is no way that any man or woman can look into another human being's heart and see for himself that the Holy Spirit lives there. The apostles couldn't do it, and neither can we, and this why the Westminster Confession (25:2) reminds us that the church on earth consists, not of *true believers,* but of those who *profess* to believe. It is not ours to judge hearts, only professions. The infallible sifting must be left to the Great Day, when the secrets of every heart will be revealed. In the meantime, we have to extend to every member of our congregation the recognition due to God's children.

Yet the Lord has not left us without criteria. Where the Spirit lives, His presence always bears fruit, and the nature of that fruit is spelled out for us in detail in Galatians 5:22-23, 'The fruit of the Spirit is love, joy, peace, patience, kindness, goodness, faithfulness, gentleness and self-control'. Beside that, we must place the love that Paul describes so memorably in 1 Corinthians 13, and which he sets forth, not as a desirable extra, or as a mark of superior Christians, but as an essential without which the most vocal and the most revered of us is but a noise.

But let's be careful. Neither of these great passages has been given to us in order to help us in judging others. In the first instance, they must be the touchstone by which we judge ourselves.

A communion of saints

The church is not, however, a mere *collection* of saints: it is a *communion* of saints or, as the original Latin form of the Creed puts it, a *communio sanctorum*. The Latin form is worth noting because the word *sanctorum* can be taken as either masculine or neuter in gender. Fortunately, we don't have to choose, but each is suggestive.

Taken as masculine, as most translations do, it denotes the communion between holy people. They communicate with each other, not only in terms of ordinary social contact, but in terms of the sort of contact Paul has in mind when he asks the Thessalonians to comfort the bereaved (I Thess. 4) and, a few moments later, tells them (not just the pastors, but the ordinary members of the church) to warn those who are out of order, encourage those who are fainthearted, and help those who are weak (I Thess. 5:13). Believers are to keep talking.

At the same time the communion of saints bespeaks partnership. For example, those who preach the gospel are in partnership with those who financially support them (I Cor. 9:11; I Tim. 5:17), and, in his letter to the Philippians, the Apostle thanks the church for its 'partnership in the gospel', speaks warmly of women who laboured side by side with him in his evangelism, and, in the next breath, refers to the rest of his fellow workers, 'whose names are in the book of life' (Phil. 4:3). Later in the same epistle, he refers to the way the church at Philippi was supporting him by their gifts during his imprisonment in Rome, making special mention of the gifts that had recently been delivered to him by their messenger, Epaphroditus. Christian labour, whatever its precise form, is always a partnership between many different individuals and many different skills.

Besides communication and partnership, the communion of saints also includes sharing, and this is the point of *sanctorum* if we take it as neuter. In the holy catholic church, there is a communion or fellowship in *holy things*. Believers have all the most important things in common: the same Father, the same Saviour, the same Spirit. We have had the same core experiences, we enjoy the same spiritual blessings, we are characterised by the same graces, and each of us has received our own appropriate measure of the gifts of the Holy Spirit, given to us, not for our personal benefit, but for the good of the whole body of Christ. Each member serves the body, each member is equipped for the service expected of her, and every member is expected to be an example to the others. Yet the whole truth is never just that the body needs us. No less truly, we need the body.

We should carefully note, however, the precise position of the 'communion of saints' within the Creed. It comes, as we have seen, after the article on the Holy Spirit, and it is immediately followed by the article on the forgiveness of sins. This order has important lessons.

First, only the Holy Spirit can make saints from sinners; and only He can nurture and mature this saintliness till, at last, we are ready for heaven.

Secondly, saints must never forget their need of forgiveness. Every day, our Father in heaven must hear the prayer, 'Forgive our debts,' coming from the hearts of men and women who are faithful penitents as well as faithful believers.

But it is not only the individual who has sins that need forgiveness. The church as institution can find peace only by believing in the forgiveness of sins, and that applies to every aspect of her existence. Her congregations, her leadership, her assemblies, convocations and councils, and her every denomination, all have sinned and come short of the glory of God. The danger here is that when we think of the church's need of forgiveness, we think only of historical sins such as, for example, her past intolerance, and her complicity in racism and the slave trade. But it's too late to call past generations to repentance. It is the sins of the church here and now that should trouble us: the hurt that *we* have caused, the way *we* have crushed the bruised reeds, the alacrity with which *we* have so quickly fallen in behind the changing standards of the world. We need forgiveness for *our* interdenominational feuding, for *our* internal strife, for *our* abandonment of the Bible as the only rule to direct us, for *our* unjustified self-confidence, for *our* carefully moderated zeal in the execution of our commission, for *our* preoccupation with reflection at the expense of action. We have to acknowledge, each of us as part of the whole, that what the Lord too often sees is not only corruption *within* the church, but corruption *of* the church. And then we have to ask, 'Lord, is it I?'

Catholicity

Finally, the church we believe in is the holy *catholic* church. This is not a biblical term, though traditionally it has been applied to the epistles of James, Peter, John and Jude, which have been described as 'catholic' epistles because, unlike the epistles of Paul, they were not addressed to particular local churches but to the whole church. It is in this sense that the term is used in the Creed. The 'catholic' church is the universal church, dispersed throughout the world, consisting of all believers, embracing all local churches, and transcending all barriers of race, nationality, language and culture.

But the term 'catholic' also describes the church which adheres to the received faith,[8] and this received more and more emphasis as successive heresies arose, rejecting the Apostolic canon, calling in question such fundamental doctrines as the deity of Christ, and setting up their own separate organisations. It was in this context that the church formulated its great creeds, not only to excommunicate such heresies, but to give a clear statement of those doctrines which it was essential to preserve.

Absolutely fundamental was the doctrine of the Trinity as set forth in the Nicene Creed (381),[9] where the church declared

---

8.   Cf. the saying attributed to Jerome, *'ecclesia ibi est ubi fides est'* ('where the faith is, there the church is').

9.   This is the slightly expanded form of the original (325) Nicene Creed which the Council of Constantinople approved in 381. Strictly speaking, it is the Nicaeno-

in terms that left no room for doubt or further controversy its belief in the eternal deity of the Son and the Holy Spirit, and the coequality of the three divine persons within the unity of the one godhead. Seventy years later, the Council of Chalcedon (451) declared, equally unambiguously, that in the one person of Christ, there are two distinct natures: He is truly and perfectly human, and truly and perfectly divine. The Apostles' Creed took a different, but no less important approach. Originally prepared, as we have seen, as the faith to be professed by all who received baptism, it put at the heart of that faith the great gospel miracles such as the Virgin Birth, the resurrection, and the ascension of Christ; the historical reality of His suffering, crucifixion, death and burial; the central Christian hope of the Lord's return; and the article we are focusing on at the moment, 'I believe in the holy catholic church.'

It would be a serious misunderstanding to view these creeds as the special preserve of Anglicanism, Romanism, and those other Christian traditions noted for their veneration for the early Fathers of the church.[10] They are rightly called the 'ecumenical creeds' because they are cherished by the whole church and express the faith of the whole church. They are thus the test of catholicity and, far from discarding them, the churches of the Reformation incorporated their substance into all the great Protestant creeds, including the Westminster Confession, the creed of world Presbyterianism. The Reformation was thus no root-and-branch break with the early church. Instead, Protestantism stayed firmly within the Nicene tradition, while at the same time bearing witness with revolutionary clarity to the doctrine of justification by faith *alone*.

Constantinopolitan Creed. It is in this expanded form that it is generally received. The most important addition was a clear affirmation of the deity of the Holy Spirit.

10.   See, for example, Calvin's comment on the creeds of the ancient councils as a whole: 'I venerate them from my heart, and would have all of them held in due honour' (*Inst.* IV:IX, 1).

It follows from this that, while no local church *is* the catholic church, every local church is part of the catholic church. This is certainly how the early churches spoke of themselves. For example, the *Letter of the Smyrneans on the Martyrdom of Polycarp* is addressed to all the 'brotherhoods of the holy and universal [catholic] Church sojourning in every place'; and Polycarp himself is referred to as bishop of 'the catholic church which is in Smyrna'.[11] And what is true of particular local churches is also true of provincial or national churches, as is recognised in the Church of Scotland Act (1921), which describes the Church of Scotland as 'part of the Holy Catholic Universal Church'.

From this point of view, every local church which adheres to the catholic faith is part of the catholic church, even though there is no longer any universally recognised earthly governance of the church. Conversely, no church or denomination which does not believe the catholic faith (the faith of the ecumenical creeds) can be regarded as part of the catholic church. They, then, have no recourse but to dismiss the whole concept of catholicity, in which case every particular church becomes an island, disrespectful towards the wisdom of the past and cut off from the living faith of the present.

But if the Reformers did not repudiate these ancient creeds, neither should the new churches which emerge from the modern missionary movement. The argument is often heard that we cannot expect the churches of Asia and Africa, with their very different cultures, to adopt the traditional creeds of the Western churches. We should remember, however, the words of Irenaeus, urging that geographical dispersion is no reason for serious variations in faith: 'For although the languages of the world are dissimilar, yet the import of the tradition is one and the same. For the Churches which have been planted in Germany do not believe or hand down

---

11.   For *The Letter of the Smyrneans on the Martyrdom of Polycarp* see *The Apostolic Fathers,* ed. J. B. Lightfoot (1891. Reprinted Grand Rapids: Baker, 1978), pp. 103-17. Polycarp was martyred A.D. 155/6.

anything different, nor do those in Spain, nor those in Gaul, nor those in the East nor those in Egypt, nor those in Libya, nor those which have been established in the central regions of the world.'[12] If the message of Jesus can be carried over from Aramaic to Greek, and from Greek to Gaelic, English and German, then the language of Nicea can be translated into Urdu, Xhosa and Japanese. Indeed, it must be so translated, because the worship of the young churches of the developing world can be sustained only if it arises from a firm belief in the eternal deity of Jesus, God's one and only Son. At the same time, the older churches must gratefully accept the gifts that Christ has given to the younger churches for the benefit of the whole body.

Conclusion

But what do the words, 'I believe,' mean when used with reference to the church? They certainly cannot mean that we are to believe whatever the church says, though it is certainly a powerful argument in support of any Christian doctrine that it has long been the unanimous belief of Christians the world over. But even Councils, such as those of Nicea and Chalcedon, which did indeed express the faith of the whole church, had no intrinsic authority, as the Westminster Confession points out.[13] Instead, all their pronouncements have to be examined in the light of Scripture. The same would apply to any future ecumenical council, but the point is purely academic, since, in the present state of the church, we can never hear one catholic voice. Instead, we have only the voices of the various denominations, whether it be Vatican Councils, Anglican Convocations, Presbyterian General Assemblies or

---

12. Irenaeus, *Against Heresies*, I:X, 2 (*The Ante-Nicene Fathers*, Vol. I, 1885. Reprinted Edinburgh, 1993); p. 331.

13. 'All synods or councils, since the Apostles' times, whether general or particular, may err; and many have erred' (*Westminster Confession*, 31:4). Cf. the *Scots Confession*, Article 20, 'As we do not rashly damn that which godly men, assembled together in general Council lawfully gathered, have proponed unto us; so without just examination dare we not receive whatsoever is obtruded unto men under the name of general Councils.'

pronouncements from the eldership of independent congregations. All may be part of the catholic church, but none speaks for it, and none has authority to lay down new doctrines or new commandments, or to bind the Christian conscience where the Holy Spirit, speaking in Scripture, has not bound it.

When we look carefully at the exact wording of the Creed, however, we find that what it is saying is not, 'I believe the church,' but, 'I believe *in* the church'; and this immediately comes as a shock. The earlier articles speak of believing *in* God the Father, of believing *in* Jesus Christ, and of believing *in* the Holy Spirit. How can, 'I believe in the church,' be part of that same sequence?

We certainly don't believe in the church in exactly the same way as we believe in Jesus. We believe in *Him* as both our Lord and Saviour: the church is neither of these, but we believe in it as the community through which divine grace reaches us, and through whose ministries and ordinances we are to grow towards maturity. We believe in the Word it preaches, in the sacraments it administers, and in the blessings that come from meeting together. We trust it to pray for us; and we trust it not as something that needs our support, but as something that supports us.

But of what church is the Creed speaking? Is it some ideal of a church; the church as she should be? No! It is speaking of the church as it actually exists: not the church invisible, without spot or wrinkle, and known only to God, but the church as we see it in our brothers and sisters: the church that is subject to both mixture and error (WC);[14] the church as it was in the Old Testament, where only a remnant were faithful, and as it was in Corinth, with its divisions and its false views of spirituality; or the one in Ephesus, which had lost the love of its early days; or Thyatira which tolerated prophets who encouraged sexual immorality. We believe in the church which is always in need of forgiveness, reform and revival. We believe in

---

14. 'The purest churches under heaven are subject to both mixture and error' (Westminster Confession, 25:5).

the church which is still only provisional, and which will not be perfect until Christ returns.

What may well be hardest of all, however, is to believe in my own church, the congregation to which I belong. Yet that, too, is part of our creed. We believe in our local church as a community of holy people, with whom we listen to the gospel being preached and with whom we share the bread and wine of the Sacrament. We believe in the church for whom we pray, and which we trust to remember us in their prayers.

It may be that ours is a church that shatters our dream of what a church should be like, but such dreams, as Bonhoeffer points out, can lead only to disillusionment: 'disillusionment with others, disillusionment with Christians in general and, if we are fortunate, disillusionment with ourselves.'[15] Faith is not asked to live in a dream world, nor is Christian brotherhood an ideal which *we* are called upon to realise: 'it is, rather, a reality created by God in Christ, in which we may participate.'[16] It is He who has made us fellow-citizens with the saints and members of the household of God, and we cannot make our participation conditional on His refurbishing His household to match our dream.

---

15. Dietrich Bonhoeffer, *Life Together* (London: SCM Press, 1954), p. 15.

16. *Ibid*, p. 18.

13

✦ THE NARROW WAY ✦

I believe, I know that I believe, I know what I believe, and I know why I believe. But I also know that faith is not a point of arrival, but a point of departure. It is our response to Christ's call, 'Follow me,' and from that moment onwards, we are pilgrims, always keeping Him in sight, and walking His Way.

Entry through a narrow gate

What is that Way?

First of all, it is a Way that can be entered only through a narrow gate (Matt. 7:13), and one clear implication of this is that we have to go through it one by one. Think of a turnstile. Thousands may go through, but each one goes through alone. The same is true of the Narrow Gate. We can't go through as groups; we have to go through as individuals, each one making their own choice of the Way and their own decision to follow Jesus. Faith and repentance are intensely personal things, and this is true even on those occasions when many go through the Gate at around the same time. Peter and his brother went through the same day (Mark 1:16-18), and yet each one went through by his own personal choice. The same was true on the Day of Pentecost. Three thousand went through the turnstile that day, but each went through in their own way and for their own reasons. Peter recognised this when he couched his closing appeal in the words, 'Repent and be baptized, *every one of you*' (Acts 2:38, italics added). It was a call for individual decision-making.

Secondly, taking the Narrow Gate means having to separate from the crowd. The issue here is that there are two gates (Matt. 7:13-14). There is a Narrow Gate leading to a Narrow Way, and there is a Wide Gate leading to a Broad Way. We clearly have a choice, but it is limited to these two options. There is no third gate, no middle way between the Narrow Way and the Broad Way. Faced with Jesus' call, we have to choose one or the other; and if we choose the Narrow Gate this immediately comes with a cost. We have to separate from the crowd, because the crowd has already opted for the Wide Gate, and they're pouring through it. If you choose the Narrow Gate, on the other hand, you'll find yourself on a lonely road because few of your former companions, and perhaps even few of your friends and loved ones, will have made your choice. They will have noticed that you've dropped out, because the step you've taken is bound to be a public one, but they won't follow you. Choosing the Narrow Gate always comes with a social cost.

Thirdly, since the Gate is narrow, we have to leave a lot of our baggage behind. Think again of the turnstile. You can get yourself through, but not your bike and your golf clubs and your six-pack. Everyone who presents at the Narrow Gate has just come off the Broad Road, still carrying the accumulations of their old lifestyle, and they cannot get them all through. Following Jesus always means turning our backs on our old lifestyle.

Remember St Paul's description of the young believers to whom he wrote his First Epistle to the Corinthians? They had shared fully in the corrupt and dissolute lifestyle of their infamous city, and the apostle draws a grim picture of what that had meant (I Cor. 6:10-11). They had been sexually immoral, idolaters, homosexuals, thieves, greedy, drunkards, revilers, swindlers. This didn't prevent their being saved, but they couldn't bring that lifestyle with them through the Gate. Salvation meant by its very nature that they had to put these things behind them, and the Apostle can claim triumphantly, 'Such *were* some of you' (I Cor. 6:11 ESV, italics added). It's what they had been, but it was no longer what they were.[1]

Not all Christians have previously led a Corinthian lifestyle. Paul himself clearly hadn't, but he still had to renounce his Pharisaism and radically revise the plan he had for his life (Phil. 3:7-11). In one form or another, this applies to every Christian's story, including the story of those who turn to Christ from a merely nominal Christian background.

Thomas Chalmers was ordained to the ministry before he had any real interest in spiritual things and, for several years, he kept his religion within very moderate bonds and famously boasted that two days a week were quite sufficient for the duties of a clergyman, leaving five days for the pursuit of any scientific study that captured his interest. But when God showed him the true state of his soul, the awful magnitude of eternity, and the solemn responsibilities of a Christian minister, everything changed. The dreams of academic preferment were left at the Gate, and he threw himself single-mindedly into promoting 'the Christian good of Scotland'. Conversion is death to moderation.

It goes without saying that those who come to the Gate from a secular-humanist background will also have to leave much behind. They bring with them all the values and mores of a society for which this present life is all, and for which the cherished goals are wealth, power, pleasure and, above all, the freedom to make their own rules.

---

1.   The same principle applies to the less lurid list of the 'works of the flesh' in Galatians 5:19-21. This list includes such sins as jealousy, fits of anger, divisiveness and envy. These, too, must be left at the Gate.

These values, manners and freedoms must all be surrendered at the Gate, and every act, thought and desire brought under subjection to Christ. Life is then bounded by what Christ sanctions, and expanded by what He promises.

When the writer to the Hebrews describes the Christian life as a race (Heb. 12:1-2), he urges his readers to lay aside not only the sins that cling to us, but every 'weight'. The race will be a challenging one, and we can ill afford to be weighed down with excess baggage.

The weights the writer has in mind are not 'sins' in the sense of practices forbidden by Scripture. They are things which hold us back in our discipleship, hinder our spiritual lives, and leave us with no energy to 'abound in the work of the Lord' (1 Cor. 15:58 ESV).[2] It is tempting to ask what exact weights the author has in mind. He's certainly not directing us to renounce all secular activity or to give up on all recreation. The secular world needs a Christian presence (Matt. 5:13-16), and our minds and our bodies need recreation. When it comes down to details, the reality is that what is no weight to one Christian may be a fatal weight to another. It may be a hobby, it may be our chosen career, it may be a friendship, it may be a particular form of entertainment, it may be the place where we live, it may be a scientific or academic pursuit (even the study of theology): the possibilities are endless. The guiding principle must be the one laid down by Paul in Philippians 1:21, 'For to me, to live is Christ.' Anything that hinders me in attempting to live such a life is a 'weight' for *me*; and I must lay it aside.

A Narrow Way

But once we've gone through the Narrow Gate, where do we find ourselves? On the Narrow Way (Matt. 7:14)![3] It is the road to which

---

2. Compare with this Jesus's words about tearing out a right eye or cutting off a right hand if either of them leads you into sin (Matt. 5:29-30).

3. Jesus does not specifically refer to it as the Narrow Way. But it is clearly contrasted with the Way that may be entered by the Wide Gate.

people have been directed by Jesus, and it's the only way to eternal life, yet it is a road little travelled, because beside it there is another called the Broad Way, which is immensely popular because it seems much the easier route. It allows great freedom of thought and action, and appeals strongly to a generation whose keynote is, 'No one tells me what I cannot do.' There are no hard 'dogmas' to believe, or challenging commandments to obey, and there is only one cardinal rule: 'Let no man (or God) tell you what to think.' You believe what you 'feel' is true for you, and you do what you 'feel' is right for you. Nor is its popularity just a matter of numbers, though it's true that far more people use it than use the Narrow Way. It's a matter of quality, too. Almost all the celebrities use it, and the beautiful people, and the successful people, and the powerful people.

The Narrow Way is very different. On this road, you aren't free to wander into strange realms of thought, neither are you free to experiment with every fashionable lifestyle. Nor again are you free to, 'Just be yourself.' Instead, your beliefs are defined by the Truth that Jesus taught, and your behaviour is defined by the clear boundaries He laid down in the Sermon on the Mount. This is the Christian Highway Code (even for pedestrians!) and it includes clear 'Must Nots' such as 'No Entry,' 'No Right Turns,' 'No U-Turns' and 'Road Closed.' On this road, it's not a matter of feeling; it's a matter of compliance with divine law. There must be no anger, no lust, no divorce, no retaliation, no judgmentalism.

But the Code also lays down clear 'Musts'. We must turn the other cheek, go the extra mile, love our enemy, and live by the Golden Rule.[4] And to these we must add such vivid models of Christian behaviour as the Parable of the Good Samaritan, with its clear warning against passing by on the other side when we come across human suffering and pain. Instead, we to whom God has

---

4. 'Whatever you wish that others would do to you, do also to them' (Matt. 7:12 ESV).

shown such mercy, must address the challenge, 'What are you going to do about it?'

But is this not perilously close to legalism, and totally at variance with Martin Luther's great doctrine of justification by faith alone: the very foundation of the gospel of free grace, assuring us that we don't have to atone for our own sins because Christ has already made full atonement for us on the cross of Calvary? Isn't this to be safeguarded at all costs? Yes, but then, in the very act of glorying in the cross, let's bear in mind the cautionary word of Dietrich Bonhoeffer, himself a loyal Lutheran: 'Luther cannot be misunderstood more grievously than by thinking that through discovering the gospel of pure grace he proclaimed a dispensation from obeying God's commandments in the world.'[5] This is entirely in line with the mind of Christ, who not only explicitly denied that He had come to abolish the Law (Matt. 5:17) but also declared that the great sign of our love for Him would be that we kept His commandments (John 14:15). The same principle lies, though much neglected, at the heart of the Great Commission, where Jesus not only directs the apostles to go and make disciples of all nations, but also charges them with teaching their new converts to 'observe all that I have commanded you'. It is precisely those who have been justified by faith who walk the Narrow Way; that Way is the Way of Holiness; and holiness is, above all, obedience.

A hard way

But the Way is not only narrow. It's also hard, for two reasons: it is the way of self-denial, and it is the way of the cross.

---

5. Dietrich Bonhoeffer, *Discipleship* (Dietrich Bonhoeffer, *Works*, Vol. 4, tr. Barbara Green and Reinhard Krauss; Minneapolis: Fortress Press, 2003, p. 49). Cf. the comments of Thomas Chalmers on the duty which ministers owe to the *converted* people in their congregation: 'The thing peculiarly suited to them is a large and explicit ministration on the *details* of holiness, the duties of faith and everyday life, and the obligations which lie upon their hearers in their relative stations as husbands, and wives, and children, and masters, and servants, and members of society' (*Institutes of Theology*; Edinburgh: Thomas Constable, 1856, Vol. II, pp. 487-80. Italics added).

First, it is the way of self-denial, as Jesus made clear: 'If anyone would come after me, let him deny himself' (Mark 8:34 ESV). This is not a matter of denying ourselves some of life's titbits, as a man might do for Lent. It's a matter of saying 'No!' to self: of renouncing self-love and the other false loves associated with it, especially the love of money and the love of pleasure (2 Tim. 3:2-4). Of course, we still have our own needs, tastes, and preferences. If we didn't, there could be no denying them. But they are no longer our priority. They have been dislodged from the place they once held by a whole new set of priorities: the credit of God's name, the advancement of His kingdom, and the doing of His will (the very things our hearts are set upon as we say the Lord's Prayer). Where Christ is Lord, self is dethroned.

And when self is dethroned, our relationship with our fellow human beings must also be revolutionised. We see others as more important than ourselves and give their needs priority over our own (Phil. 2:3-4). We are, after all, walking Christ's way, and His way was to make others rich even when that meant making Himself poor (2 Cor. 8:9). He sat loose to His own rights, and focused instead on the glory of His Father and the needs of a lost world.

Yet we are not presented with a set of self-denials from which we are expected to make a selection. We make one life-changing choice: to follow Jesus. The self-denial will follow.[6] The disciples didn't need to go looking for trials or deprivations. They came just because they were with the Master, as He himself pointed out: 'You are those who have stayed with me in my trials' (Luke 22:28 ESV). After all, they were following a man who had nowhere to lay His head: a Rabbi who was hated and despised by all the people who mattered. It wasn't their personal choice to put their lives at risk in a

---

6. It also arises from coming face to face with the truth about ourselves. C. S. Lewis has left a vivid description of what he discovered when he first examined himself seriously: 'I found,' he wrote, 'what appalled me; a zoo of lusts, a bedlam of ambitions, a nursery of fears, a harem of fondled hatreds. My name was legion' (*Surprised by Joy: The Shape of my Early Life*; 1955. Reprinted London: Fontana, 1960), p. 181. It's hard to continue worshipping yourself once you've looked in such a mirror.

storm on the Sea of Galilee (Mark 4:35-41). They just happened to be with Him and, even after His Ascension, the mere fact of being His followers would regularly mean having to make a choice between their own comfort and convenience on the one hand, and loyalty to the Lord on the other. Saul of Tarsus was chosen to suffer many things for Jesus' sake (Acts 9:16), but he wasn't told what forms these sufferings would take. They would come unsought as he lived in obedience to the heavenly vision (Acts 26:19).

The same is true of every believer. When the Writer to the Hebrews describes the Christian life as a race (Heb. 12:1), he makes plain that we don't choose the course. We have to follow the one laid out for us; if it isn't left to us to choose the course, neither do we choose the obstacles, or even the position of the finishing-line. All we are told is that the race will demand great powers of endurance (AV, 'patience,') and tax our spiritual stamina to its limits. Beyond that, we are in the hands of the Course Designer:

> Thy way, not mine, O Lord
> However dark it be;
> Lead me by thine own hand,
> Choose out the path for me.
>
> (HORATIUS BONAR, 1808–89)[7]

This is not a matter of us handing control over to God. He *is* in control, and always has been. It is a matter of recognising it and trusting Him to work everything together for our good (Rom. 8:28).

The Way of the cross

Secondly, the Way is hard because it is the Way of the Cross. But just as in the case of self-denial, bearing the cross is not a second

---

7. Cf. Newman's lines in the hymn *Lead Kindly Light*:
    The night is dark, and I am far from home;
    Lead Thou me on.
    Keep Thou my feet; I do not ask to see
    The distant scene: one step enough for me.

additional decision following upon the decision to follow Christ. It is inseparable from being one of His people, one of His crowd, and Jesus' original hearers, all too familiar with public crucifixions, would have realised immediately what He meant. He didn't mean what we commonly mean today when we use such platitudes as, 'Everyone has his own cross to bear.' Nor was He merely saying that Christians will have their fair share of life's troubles. The cross was an instrument of execution and, as we see from Jesus' own case (John 19.17), the condemned criminal had to carry his own cross to the place of punishment. What Jesus was saying was that becoming one of His disciples was tantamount to signing your own death warrant – and it was no empty warning. At least two of His original hearers, James and Peter, both paid the ultimate price for following Jesus, as did Stephen and Paul; and there is solemn truth in James Denney's observation that 'the typical Christian is the martyr'.[8] The ferocity of persecution will vary from place to place and from time to time,[9] but the unvarying reality, as declared by the Lord Himself, is that the world will hate His followers as it hated Him (John 15:18). Its great religions and its powerful despotisms see in Christ a potent threat to their own future, close their doors against Christian missions, and move quickly to eradicate the first green shoots of Christianity. And even the self-consciously tolerant Western democracies fear the threat posed to human freedom, especially sexual freedom, by Christian ethics. For the time being, they shrink from bringing down on Christian belief the full force of criminal law, but they are clearly committed to closing down its space and, above all, to denying it a voice in the public square.

---

8. James Denney, *Jesus and the Gospel*, (Hodder and Stoughton, 1909), p. 234.

9. Cf. Paul's warning that 'in the last days perilous times shall come' (2 Tim. 3:1, AV). But note, too, John Stott's comment, 'What Timothy is to understand about the last days is not that they are uniformly, continuously evil, but that they will include "perilous seasons"' (*Guard the Gospel: The Message of 2 Timothy*; London: Inter-Varsity Press, 1973, p. 83). The phrase, 'the last days,' refers, of course to the whole period between the first and the second advent of Christ.

Christians should never court persecution, nor provoke it. Our duty is to stick close to Jesus and then take what comes. But as he takes his first step, let the pilgrim be warned: the world will not admire him for his piety or honour him as a pillar of society. Divine restraint may set bounds to its hostility and scorn, but everyone who walks through the Narrow Gate runs the risk of being treated as the Master was treated.

14

✢ FOLLOWING THE GOOD ✢ SHEPHERD

But is there nothing more to be said about Jesus' Way than that it is a narrow way and a hard way?

There is indeed! It is the way that leads to life; while we walk it, goodness and mercy follow us all our days; when the journey is over, we will dwell in the house of the Lord for ever.

These are the familiar sentiments of the Twenty-third Psalm. It is often referred to as 'the Shepherd Psalm' and that title is entirely appropriate, since the overarching theme is the care of the Good Shepherd for His sheep. However hard the road may be, we have the reward of being with Jesus. But it is no dishonour to the shepherd-theme to suggest that the Psalm could equally well be called 'the Pilgrim Psalm', especially if we remember that, in the East, the shepherd went before the flock, and the sheep followed. This is exactly the Christian experience. We are responding to Jesus' call, 'Follow me,' and the Twenty-third Psalm is a description of the changing scenes through which the Good Shepherd leads us. The way may be hard, and fraught, yet this is an immensely privileged flock, and not all the privileges are reserved till the journey is over.

The Shepherd

The first and most obvious privilege is the Shepherd Himself: 'the LORD is my shepherd.' To the psalmist, as he penned these words, the Shepherd was Jehovah, the God of Israel:[1] the one who had created the heavens and the earth, brought His people out of Egypt, and led them through the Red Sea. He was also the God who is 'merciful and gracious, slow to anger and abounding in steadfast love' (Ps. 103:8 ESV). This is the one to whom David points as his shepherd, and he was not the only Old Testament prophet to strike this note. One of Isaiah's most memorable passages speaks of God in similar terms:

> He will tend his flock like a shepherd;
>> he will gather the lambs in his arms;
> he will gather them in his bosom.
>> and gently lead those who are with young
>>>> (Isa. 40:11 ESV).

But when we as Christians sing this psalm, we do so, not only with the light of the Old Testament, but also in the light of the New, and especially in the brilliant light of the Incarnation. In Jesus, the Lord our Shepherd has taken our human nature, lived among us, shared our experiences, and personally walked the Narrow Way. He is thus able to feel with us in all our weaknesses and to understand every trial we have to go through (Heb. 4:15). Nothing that was human was alien to Him.

This is why in Revelation 7:17, we have the remarkable picture of the church, the flock of Christ, being shepherded by a lamb: 'The

---

1. The current convention among scholars is to pronounce the sacred Name as Yahweh, but the name Jehovah is so firmly established in tradition (and in Christian worship) that it would be pedantic to use Yahweh in the current context, especially as there is no certainty about the original pronunciation.

Lamb in the midst of the throne will be their shepherd' (ESV).[2] The flock can never say, 'He has no feeling for us. He has no idea what it's like to be a sheep.' On the contrary, He is like us in every way (Heb. 2:17): not only in the sense that He has personal experience of our natural human limitations, but that He spared Himself none of the stresses and pressures that mark the lives of His 'friends' (John 15:13).

But there is one detail in which the New Testament does not surpass the clarity of the Old: David's description of the LORD as not only 'our' shepherd, but as 'my' shepherd. It is as if each sheep had the Shepherd all to herself and enjoyed His undivided attention. This concurs with what we read in John 10:3,14: the Good Shepherd knows each sheep by name. This is true, of course, in normal day-to-day shepherding. To most of us (and I include myself), all sheep look the same. We cannot tell one from the other. But the good shepherd can. He recognises each face and knows each history – and what is true of the human shepherd is pre-eminently true of the divine. He has a vast flock, too big for any man to count (Rev. 7:9), yet He knows the name of each, never forgets a face, and never confuses one with another.

Nor is this a knowledge He has acquired but lately. He has known each sheep from eternity (Rom. 8:29), always loved it, always had a plan for it, and always purposed to lay down His life for it (Gal. 2:20).[3] And however weak they may be, however prone to wander and go astray, however tempted to give up, He will bring each one safely home.

But the sheep have to walk there, and what the Twenty-third Psalm does, is to give us a picture of the sheep on their journey. It begins with an idyllic picture of a flock which lacks nothing. The road no longer feels hard. Instead, the flock lies down in green pastures, to

---

2. The Greek, *poimanei*, which the AV translated 'shall feed,' is the verb form of the noun *poimēn*, a shepherd.

3. Galatians 2:20, 'I live by faith in the Son of God, who loved me and gave himself for me.'

the soothing sound of gently-flowing water, enjoying a time of rest and recovery; for the moment, the way is smooth and easy.

The Good Shepherd doesn't drive His sheep relentlessly. In every Christian life, there are moments of rest and refreshing: times when we enjoy full assurance of God's love and forgiveness, receive clear answers to our prayers, draw fresh vigour from the fellowship of His people, feast on His Word, and rejoice with 'joy unspeakable and full of glory' (I Pet. 1:8 KJV).

Who's to say what proportion of our days will be of this kind? But they will not be few, and we must be careful lest, like the spies sent out to do a reconnaissance of the Promised Land, we bring back an evil report, as if the Narrow Way were an unrelieved assault course, and as if the Good Shepherd had nothing to offer but 'blood, toil, tears and sweat.' We must tell as it is, and even on this side of heaven, 'as it is' includes green pastures and still waters. We have the best shepherd in the world, He leads us through the finest spiritual scenery in the world, and He gives us the best provision and the best protection in the world.

The Valley of Deathly Darkness

But then suddenly the scene changes, and we see the flock being led through what has traditionally been called 'the Valley of the Shadow of Death'. The psalmist is not thinking here specifically of times of bereavement, or of his own deathbed, overwhelming though these may seem to be. Nor is he thinking of some terrifying psychological experience. On the contrary, he is determined that if and when he has to walk through this valley, he will do so without fear.

The picture is nevertheless a grim one. He imagines himself in a narrow ravine of deathly darkness, where unknown and unseen dangers lurk. It is not a picture of ordinary trials and stresses. It is a picture of extremes, but it is a picture, and not one easily reduced to words. It must be left to speak for itself, though we may not even recognise it when we come to it. We certainly have no warrant to people it, as Bunyan did, with fiends, hob-goblins and satyrs of the pit; or to place the Valley so close to the mouth of Hell that the pilgrim can hear its roar and see its flames.[4] Bunyan himself certainly had such vivid experiences, but they probably owed more to his own neuroses than to the unavoidable features of the Narrow Way. Bunyan does indeed say that the Valley was unavoidable, because the road to heaven leads this way, and this is true to the extent that the road will always lead through what John Newton called 'many dangers, toils and snares.' But this doesn't mean that every follower of Jesus is going to have close personal encounters with the demonic or go through periods in his life where he feels as if he were walking on the brink of Hell.

In fact, the psalmist's real interest is not in the Valley and its details. His focus is still on the prowess and vigilance of his Shepherd. Even in the worst imaginable (or even unimaginable) scenario he need have no fear because, however dark and claustrophobic the ravine, however inescapable the dangers, however deadly his foes, the Shepherd will never be far away: 'I will fear no evil, for *you* are with me' (v. 4). The Good Shepherd, the Supreme Pastor (Heb. 13:20) will always be there, and faith hears Him moving and feels His touch. He knows the Valley, having been through it Himself; and every lamb is precious to Him because He paid for it with His life. He never loses one.

We should note, however, that here David is facing only a possibility. He is not in the Valley, and he is not yet being asked to cope. Did he keep his resolution, and come through everything without fear? There were certainly moments when he was hardly a model of composure and resolve, and Scripture has kept a faithful record of these for the encouragement of more ordinary mortals.[5]

---

4. Bunyan's description of the Valley of the Shadow of Death is to be found in *The Pilgrim's Progress* of which, of course, there are many editions. But it needs to be read in the light of his searing spiritual autobiography, *Grace Abounding to the Chief of Sinners*, of which, again, there are multiple editions.

5. In Psalm 22, for example, he feels forsaken and rejected; in Psalm 69 he speaks of himself as sinking in a deep mire where there is no foothold, and where he

But even if David's courage did sometimes fail, and his faith desert him,[6] what matters is that the Shepherd *was* always with him; and even when faith cannot see Him it should know that, though the darkness may hide Him from us, it can never hide us from Him.

A banquet in the presence of His foes

But the Valley is not a cul-de-sac: as surely as there was a way in, so there is a way out, and David moves on. But though the Valley is now behind him, his troubles are not over. Instead, the next scene shows him surrounded by enemies but, as with the Valley, it is not the enemies as such that interest him. What he wants to highlight is that, despite being surrounded by dangerous foes, God entertains him as an oriental monarch would entertain a guest. He anoints his head with oil and prepares a banquet, and, as befits a banquet, David's cup is soon running over. We don't know who the foes were, and the psalm offers no details as to the cup,[7] but the central point is clear: the hostility of the world, even at its worst, cannot prevent God from entertaining His people right royally, and giving them cause for celebration.

Christian joy doesn't depend on circumstances. Paul and Silas didn't wait till their circumstances changed: they sang their hymns while still in the deepest dungeon, their feet fast in the stocks. Nor is it mere romance to say that it was often when persecution was at its height that the church has received the most abundant

---

has grown weary of crying out to God; and in Psalm 88, one of the Sons of Korah compares himself to those whom God remembers no more. It must be emphasised, once again, that these are not universal Christian experiences, but it must also be emphasised that no believer who has had them should conclude that he is therefore not a Christian at all.

6. See, for example, the Lord's question to His terrified disciples during the storm on the Sea of Galilee, 'Where is your faith?' (Luke 8:25). They had it, but they weren't applying it to their predicament.

7. The closest parallels are (1) in Psalm 116:13, where the psalmist speaks of taking the 'cup of salvation/s', and (2) the Lord's reference at the Last Supper to the cup as 'my blood of the covenant' (Matt. 26:28). Objectively, the cup flows over with the blessings secured by the Blood; subjectively, it is the cup of overflowing gratitude.

answers to her prayers, the unity of believers has been most evident, and the power of the gospel most triumphant. On the moors of south-western Scotland in the seventeenth century, the threat of Claverhouse's dragoons never deprived the Covenanters of their gospel-feasts; neither did slavery take the music out of the African Christians condemned to life on the plantations of North America; nor did the gulags of Stalin and Kruschev crush the life out of Russia's unregistered churches. And what has been true of churches has also been true of individuals. God can put melody in the hearts of His people even in the darkest circumstances. We must pray for it.

Goodness and mercy all his days

By the time we come to the last verse of the Psalm, the Valley and the enemies are no longer in sight. Instead, the psalmist is assured that goodness and mercy will follow him all the days of his life. The future tense is used: God's love will never let go; or as Jesus puts it in John 10:28-29, we are held in two almighty hands, those of the Father and those of the Son, and no one can ever snatch us out of such hands. But forward-looking though the words are, they also reflect David's lifelong experience. Goodness and love *have* followed him all the days of his life;[8] and St Paul bears the same witness, when he declares in Romans 8:28 that he 'knows' (as a matter of personal experience) that God works all things together for the good of those who love Him. Even the Valley of Deathly Darkness was part of God's 'bright design'.

In God's house for evermore

But what about when these days are over, and the pilgrimage draws to its close? It will be but the End of the Beginning, because the relationship between the psalmist and Jehovah can never be broken,

---

8. The word for 'love' in Psalm 23:6 is *hesed*, meaning specifically God's steadfast covenant-love, implying loyalty and commitment as well as affection. It has followed David all the days of his life, as his Psalms abundantly testify.

not even by death. He will dwell in the house of the Lord for ever. Some would limit this to a wish on the psalmist's part to spend his remaining days in God's earthly house. But David (and we have no reason to doubt that he was the author) never spent all his days in God's earthly house. He spent many of them on the field of battle, and any attempt to confine the reference to the Temple, founders on the fact that it wasn't even built in David's day. Even after it was built, no later psalmist ever spent all his days there. In any case, the psalmist is not expressing a wish. He is setting forth a certainty. He will dwell in the house of the Lord for ever.

We must read these words in the light of God's full and final revelation, and, when we do this, we realise the perfect accord between Jesus' account of the Narrow Way and the psalmist's picture of the Shepherd's Way. According to the psalmist, the Shepherd's Way leads to God's house; according to Jesus, the Narrow Way leads to Life (Matt. 7:14), and by that he means not merely a continuation of life as we now know it, but life more abundant (John 10:10), or life to the full. It means life for the soul in a blessed immortality, but it also means life for the body in a glorious resurrection. It means a life where the image of God, defaced in Adam, is gloriously restored; a life where we have the strength of body and the acuteness of mind to serve God as He deserves; a life where we share in Christ's dominion over a new world; a life where we enjoy for ever the pastoral care of the Lamb (Rev. 7:17); a life where, with clearer faith and purer heart, we see Christ as He is, and in Him see God face to face.

This takes the psalmist's 'green pastures and still waters' to a whole new level. But the last word on 'God's house' must come, surely, from Jesus. It is His Father's house. From it He had come, to it He would return, and on the eve of His return, He spoke of it warmly. It is, He says, a house of many rooms; and it would need to be, because the Father has a huge number of children gathered from every nation, tribe, people, and language (Rev. 7:9). The disciples were clearly troubled (John 14:1) by the thought that Jesus was leaving them to return to His Father, and fearful that there would be no room for them where He was going. The Lord hastens to reassure them. There are many rooms: enough for them all, and for multitudes more.[9] But He assures them, too, that He Himself will be there to welcome them; not only so, but He will receive them to His own quarters (v. 3 ESV), 'that where I am, there you may be also.'

Where? It can only be the glory He had with the Father before the world existed (John 17:5)! What this means we cannot say till we actually see the House. All we know is that 'God's house' is where Christ lives; shortly after He went home, the disciples, one by one, followed Him; and what was true of them will be true of every one who goes through the Narrow Gate. 'We nightly pitch our moving tent, a day's march nearer home.'

But in the meantime, Jesus told the Twelve, He had to go to prepare it for them. This is challenging. Was it not already ready when David had gone home, hundreds of years before? Had it not, indeed, been 'prepared' before the foundation of the world (Matt. 25:34)? Yes, in the eternal foreordination of God, but there was still one momentous detail to be added. There was a vacant place in the centre of the Throne. The Lamb had not yet taken His seat. Yes, He had been with the Father from all eternity, but not in our nature. The dust of the earth had yet to take His place at God's right hand, holding the sceptre, and opening the Scroll (Rev. 5:6-7).

It's easy to imagine David eagerly anticipating the arrival of his greater Son, and now that He's there as the ascended Lord, the

---

9.   At this point in his *Homilies on the Gospel of John* (Tractate XVII), Augustine introduces the idea that 'the many mansions point to the different grades of merit in that one eternal life. The saints, like the stars in the sky, obtain in the kingdom different mansions of diverse degrees of brightness' (*NPNF*, 1st series, Vol. VII, p. 321). But such a thought is quite alien to the context, and Calvin rightly dismisses it as erroneous: 'He says that the mansions are many, not that they are different or unlike, but that there are sufficient for a great number; as if He had said that there is room there, not only for Himself, but for all his disciples' (*The Gospel According to St John 11-21*, p. 74).

house is fully illuminated: 'the Glory of God did lighten it, and the Lamb is the light thereof' (Rev. 21:23, AV). The table is laid afresh, but now with the incarnate Christ at its head. Our cup runs over, and every creature in heaven, on earth and in the sea, breaks into song, 'To him who sits on the throne and to the Lamb be blessing and honour and glory and might forever and ever!' (Rev. 5:13 ESV). Amen!

Also available from Christian Focus Publications...

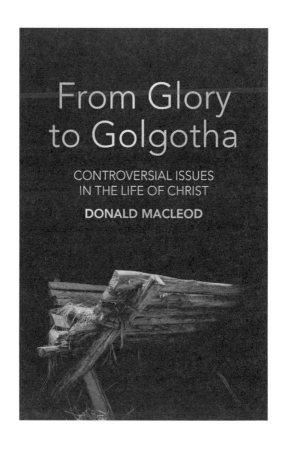

From Glory to Golgotha

CONTROVERSIAL ISSUES
IN THE LIFE OF CHRIST

DONALD MACLEOD

ISBN 978-1-5271-0636-9

From Glory to Golgotha

Controversial Issues in the Life of Christ

Donald Macleod

Renowned theologian and author, Donald Macleod explains controversial topics from the life of Christ with clarity and care. Staying true to the biblical text he points readers to reflect on the Saviour who has captivated his own heart and mind. This new edition includes 4 new chapters, originally published as articles on the Desiring God website.

Drawing on over 60 years of Biblical research, Donald Macleod is somehow able to magnificently and adoringly expound the mysteries of Christ with a skill which will not only educate, but draw his readers closer to the unfathomable realities of what God did in sending His Son.

Iver Martin
Principal, Edinburgh Theological Seminary, Edinburgh, Scotland

... passion and intensity, decades of study, deep theological reflection and serious polemical interaction, and even more, the heart of a believing theologian who knows he needs Christ and His Cross. If your prayer is 'more love to Thee, O Christ,' here is fuel for your devotion. Read and believe and worship.

Ligon Duncan
Chancellor and CEO, Reformed Theological Seminary

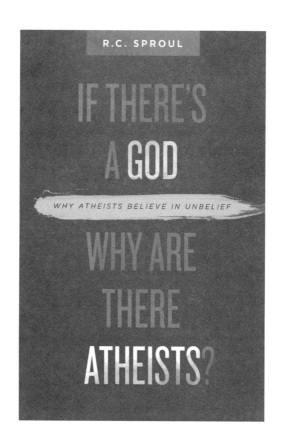

R.C. SPROUL

IF THERE'S
A GOD

WHY ATHEISTS BELIEVE IN UNBELIEF

WHY ARE
THERE
ATHEISTS?

ISBN 978-1-5271-0105-0

If There's a God Why Are There Atheists?

Why Atheists Believe in Unbelief

R. C. SPROUL

A common charge levelled against people with religious beliefs in general, and with Christian convictions in particular, is that their beliefs are motivated not by reasonable evidence but by psychological needs. In fact, many respected people, accepting the arguments of atheist thinkers, believe that psychology and the social sciences have explained away religion.

Engaging with these thinkers' works on a psychological as well as theological basis, Sproul shows that there are as many psychological and sociological explanations for unbelief as for belief – and that atheistic conclusions should not be accepted blindly.

For the believer who is troubled by doubts or who wants to respond intelligently to unbelievers, it offers clear, thought-provoking analysis. For the unbeliever who has an open mind, it offers stimulating debate, worthy of time and thought.

Christian Focus Publications

Our mission statement –

STAYING FAITHFUL
In dependence upon God we seek to impact the world through literature faithful to His infallible Word, the Bible. Our aim is to ensure that the Lord Jesus Christ is presented as the only hope to obtain forgiveness of sin, live a useful life and look forward to heaven with I Iim.

Our books are published in four imprints:

CHRISTIAN
FOCUS

Popular works including biographies, commentaries, basic doctrine and Christian living.

CHRISTIAN
HERITAGE

Books representing some of the best material from the rich heritage of the church.

MENTOR

Books written at a level suitable for Bible College and seminary students, pastors, and other serious readers. The imprint includes commentaries, doctrinal studies, examination of current issues and church history.

CF4•K

Children's books for quality Bible teaching and for all age groups: Sunday school curriculum, puzzle and activity books; personal and family devotional titles, biographies and inspirational stories – because you are never too young to know Jesus!

Christian Focus Publications Ltd,
Geanies House, Fearn, Ross-shire,
IV20 1TW, Scotland, United Kingdom.
www.christianfocus.com